Raising Your Game

Ethan J. Skolnick and Dr. Andrea Corn

Raising Your Game

Over 100 accomplished athletes help you
guide your girls and boys through sports

iUniverse LLC
Bloomington

Raising Your Game
Over 100 accomplished athletes help you
guide your girls and boys through sports

iUniverse books may be ordered through booksellers or by contacting:

iUniverse LLC
1663 Liberty Drive
Bloomington, IN 47403
www.iuniverse.com
1-800-Authors (1-800-288-4677)

ISBN: 978-1-4759-6087-7 (sc)
ISBN: 978-1-4759-6088-4 (hc)
ISBN: 978-1-4759-6089-1 (ebk)

Library of Congress Control Number: 2012921004

Printed in the United States of America

iUniverse rev. date: 08/01/2013

CONTENTS

PREFACE

Dr. Andrea Corn

I wish this book were around when I was growing up.

Perhaps I would not have seen it or read it. Perhaps, however, my parents would have come across a copy.

Perhaps they would have flipped through the pages, searching for athletes or circumstances they recognized. Perhaps a careful study of the subject matter that most interested them would have made a difference— for them and for me. Perhaps it would have compelled them to alter the way they approached my youth sports experience.

Perhaps that would have helped me feel less alone and more at ease in athletic settings.

My parents certainly meant well. They loved me, and they were the ones who instilled my initial love for sports. My most cherished memories revolve around Cardinals baseball and hearing Harry Caray and Jack Buck call games on KMOX. My father, a good athlete who had coached a middle school football squad to a state championship, took me to see all four St. Louis professional teams. I admired his talent and knowledge, and conversing about sports became our most comfortable way to connect.

My mother especially enjoyed tennis, which, before Title IX, was one of the few respectable sports for young girls. I adored the game from my first grip of a racket, spending hours practicing my strokes, whether against the garage door or a concrete wall at a nearby high school.

My family moved to South Florida when I was fifteen, and tennis became my salvation during a difficult and unhappy adjustment. As a junior, I made the Miami Beach Senior High squad and watched our team's top-ranked players win the state championship. My progression, however, had its limits. My toughest opponent was never on the other side of the net; it was within. I was passionate but not fearless, restricted by a gnawing sensation. I couldn't quite articulate how or why, but I knew I wasn't being put in the best possible position to reach my potential.

As I lost matches, I continued losing more of myself. My parents tried to help in the best way they knew how. They provided lessons, thinking that practice and repetition would strengthen my game. Sadly it wasn't sufficient. It couldn't overcome our communication breakdown— my difficulty in expressing my insecurities, combined with my parents' difficulty in acknowledging, understanding, and addressing what I *did* express. Again and again my doubts and fears simply got swept aside. My parents did so not out of malice but in an ill-fated attempt to do anything to minimize my distress. I did so because that was what I had been taught: if I couldn't eliminate my discomfort and find a way to please myself, I would try to please others. I continued to take this trouble to the court, and my trouble rallying on the court served to compound it.

I did rally later in life. After a painful divorce involving two young children, I underwent therapy and then analysis. That helped me reconcile what had transpired in my youth, on and off the court. I learned to understand myself from the inside out; how to make sense of all feeling states without dismissing or devaluing them; how to hear and process my feelings and their insightful messages; how to face fears and embrace the healing power of self-acceptance.

I have, after many years, found some peace.

I have found my voice.

I now draw upon my own experiences to help young people and young athletes draw out whatever may be churning inside—and to help adults guide them through that process. I do so through private therapy, public appearances, and published work. I created and hosted a radio program directed at teenagers and have written articles and editorials for *South Florida Parenting*, the National Association for Youth Sports, and the Association for Applied Sports Psychology (AASP), as well as the *New York Times* and the *South Florida Sun-Sentinel*.

I still play tennis, participating in competitive singles as well A2 league doubles. Even when my A game is absent, I can still succeed, relying upon my mental and emotional stability. I stay present-minded, play to the best of my ability, and focus on what is within my control—no more, no less. I am proud of how far I've come, but I know that many children on courts and fields across America are as I was and still have a long way to go. And I know that many parents are like my parents, hoping to help but not fully understanding how.

That is why it meant so much for me to write this unique book, along with Ethan who has brought to life—with his interviews and prose— the vision I have carried in my heart for years. Together we believe we have produced something quite unique, something that relies upon dozens of recognizable and respected voices from a variety of athletic and family backgrounds, something that brings the material to life in a manner missing from much of youth sports and parenting literature. This book is a hybrid, interspersing athletes' anecdotes with time-tested psychoanalytic and sports psychology concepts in a way that coaches parents to consider what really matters. No athlete could have ever predicted or envisioned how youth sports participation would transform his or her life. That can only be done with reflection, reviewing where the enduring values and lessons were learned and what could have been done differently and proceeding forward with thoughtful intentions for their own children.

My co-author and I want to mention three quick asides:

First, *Raising Your Game* will often address the reader in the second person, but we fully recognize that these days "you" could be something other than a biological parent. You could be a grandparent. You could be a stepparent or adoptive parent. You could be an uncle or an aunt. You could be an older sibling or cousin. You could be unrelated but still in position, in some way, to positively influence a child's youth sports experience. And, yes, you could even be the coach, and we do focus plenty of attention on how coaches should conduct themselves. However, we are mainly concerned with helping the primary caregivers—of all the types mentioned above—work in collaboration *with* those coaches for the benefit of the child.

Second, and in that same vein, the title should not be misconstrued as a call for a child to raise his or her level of play. If this book gives you some ideas about how to assist athletic performance, that is all the better. Yet the mission is to get you to raise *your* game in terms of the guidance you provide in every area of a child's experience.

Third, the athletes' interviews were conducted from 2008 through 2012, so some part of their circumstances and attitudes may have changed over the course of that time, or since. Sports, after all, are an evolving journey, not a destination, and that is especially true for youth sports.

Our recommendation is that the youth sports journey not be taken alone but rather with an adult serving as a child's teammate—a winning tie. The two can strengthen their connection through enrichment and enjoyment. Here's hoping this book raises your awareness and, in turn, helps you raise your game.

ACKNOWLEDGMENTS

ANY PROJECT that requires more than four years to complete also requires plenty of patience, not only on the part of the collaborators but also on the part of those around them. So we wish to start by thanking our respective spouses, Stephen Corn and Carolina Skolnick, for their understanding of the many hours that we met to write, rewrite, and, yes, rewrite this book.

We also thank many members of our families, starting with Andrea's parents, Janet and Julian Sincoff, and Ethan's parents, Shelley and Louis, for indulging our love of sports from an early age and for all the car rides to the athletic activities that we enjoyed. We thank our siblings, Andrea's brother, Gregg, and Ethan's brother, Seth, for serving as our childhood practice partners and for continuing to do so even after our behavior didn't necessarily warrant it. Andrea thanks her children, Jennifer and Josh, for giving her so many chances to feel like a proud parent, whether watching their performances on stage or on the field. We thank Dr. Jan Bell at St. Thomas University for allowing Andrea to teach in the sports administration program, which resulted in our introduction, with Ethan invited as a guest speaker. We thank many friends and colleagues for their advice, which led to constructive changes in direction. We even thank Panera Bread for its many franchises down the Federal Highway corridor in South Florida, providing convenient places to work as well as an awards card for the occasional discounted soup or sandwich.

Mostly, though, we heartily thank the athletes we interviewed, not only for their time but also for their honesty. We encourage readers to research and support their philanthropic endeavors, so many of which do so much good for children.

INTRODUCTION: "IT WAS SO FUN!"

Two grown men had just engaged in some serious business: a structured shootaround for their professional basketball team, the Miami Heat, arguably the most scrutinized squad in the sports world and one that happened to be headed toward the 2012 NBA championship.

It took little to transform **LeBron James** and **Dwyane Wade** into carefree kids.

Just a simple question before they boarded the bus back to the hotel:

What did they play as children?

In a flash James and Wade transported themselves back two decades, to the often unforgiving urban environments of Akron and Chicago, respectively, when they weren't yet the international icons that so many have since come to cheer and boo and know.

Rather, they were young children from broken homes, finding a way to overlook and even overcome their challenging circumstances by finding freedom, creativity, escape, and joy …

In play.

Uncomplicated, unsupervised, improvised, innocent play.

"We played a game called free frog," James said, smiling. "You throw the ball up, and whoever grabs it gets to run for the touchdown. You'd play basketball on any court that you could find outdoors. You'd just try to find any sport. Kickball, that was probably the number-one game all us kids played."

"Kickball," Wade broke in, eyes alight. "So much fun."

"Kickball, yeah," James said. "That was the best game, because you don't need much. All you need is a dirt field, and you can find anything

7

to make as bases, and you just go for it. Because for us underprivileged kids, we didn't have basketballs all the time; we didn't have courts; we didn't have footballs all the time. So find you a little *kickball*; you can make a kickball anything."

"I'm going to tell you one of the funnest games I played," Wade said, his language as loose as it was then. "In school we had a game called VBB. It was volleyball, basketball, and baseball. So you start off at the plate hitting it like a volleyball, right?"

"Right?" James said.

Wade explained that after the batter "punched" the volleyball, he had to run the bases.

"The point is, he's got to get home," Wade said.

Even if the batter sent the ball all the way to the stage, on the other side of the gym, it wasn't really a home run; if it went that far, those in the "field" were still allowed to retrieve it.

"That's where the basketball comes in, right?" Wade said rhetorically.

"Right," James said.

The team in the field needed to pass the ball three times before the third catcher could shoot it through the basket—all before the runner touched home plate.

That last part? Not surprisingly, given what he would later choose as a career, that was Wade's specialty.

"I was nice," Wade said. "I was the one they always tried to find to shoot the shot. So somebody would say 'one, two,' and then throw it to me for three, and I would shoot it. I was nice in the field. Yeah. Oh, I used to drain people! One, two, three! Wow! It was so fun!"

Fun.

That concept will be the focus of this book.

That is what sometimes gets lost in youth sports, which may explain why so many kids drop out. According to a landmark study in 1991, over 70 percent of children quit before turning thirteen, and most observers believe the percentage has increased since.[1]

"Encourage, support, and be there for them. If you make it fun, you've got a better chance for a kid to gravitate toward sports," two-time NBA Most Valuable Player **Steve Nash** said. "And hopefully away from some other things."

Fun.

That was the word present and prominent in nearly every conversation with those we chose to guide you through the youth sports experience, from the earliest and least-structured activity to the more advanced stages of pressurized competition.

We chose accomplished athletes.

We chose them to guide us, a sportswriter and a child/adolescent psychologist, in our aim to guide you. Over the course of four years, we sought stories and suggestions from nearly 150 of these athletes, male and female, professional and amateur, current and former, and from different generations, economic circumstances, ethnic backgrounds, and family structures. We targeted these athletes as interview subjects not because we aimed to glorify their exploits, expected any child to replicate their extreme and unlikely success, or even deemed the pursuit of such a goal to be the fundamental purpose of playing.

We interviewed these athletes for their expertise and advice.

Because they know.

They know what it feels like to be a kid, which often means not knowing very much. Not knowing which sport to choose. Not knowing which role models to follow. Not knowing how to master a new skill.

---

1   Study of Youth Sports, Michigan State University.

Not knowing how to impress a coach. Not knowing how to please a parent. Not knowing how to talk to a teammate. Not knowing one's own body—its potential and its limitations. Not knowing the long-term payoff of present challenges. Not knowing if sports are even worth the trouble anymore.

And now many of them are in a position to know something else too.

They know how you feel as a parent.

They know because they are parents themselves.

They know why so many children are signed up for youth sports, with more than thirty million of those age sixteen or under participating each year in organized athletic programs not sponsored by schools—and many, many others playing on teams at school.[2] They know better than anyone the value of sports and all those lessons and advantages that went beyond riches or fame.

"The dividends are huge for a parent whose kids play sports," Nash said. "It's such an educational tool, such a growth vehicle for young people who participate in sports. It's great for health and wellness."

Parents sign up their kids to keep them active, busy, and physically fit, especially in light of the modern obesity epidemic.

Parents sign up their kids to learn to follow rules, respect authority, cooperate with peers, solve problems, and handle adversity. They sign up their kids to increase the understanding of the value of hard work and practice, by seeing it translate into skill development. They sign up their kids to compete, giving them an opportunity to encounter, and appropriately respond to, both victory and defeat.

Parents sign up their sons ... and their daughters.

"Just the sheer number of girls that are participating now is exponentially more than when I was a kid," said **Brandi Chastain**, who

---

2   Greg Bach, Communications Director for the National Alliance for Youth Sports

scored the game-winning goal in the 1999 Women's World Cup. "I think also the acceptance of girls participating in sports [has increased]."

They sign up their kids, above all, to provide a forum for fun.

"Especially at a young age," Hall of Fame quarterback **Dan Marino** said.

Like Marino had, way back when, before he knew what he would become.

These elite athletes also know something else from their childhood and adolescent experiences. They know that "signing up" is not sufficient. They know how much you, as the adult looking after the child, matter. They know that while you are making the right call by exposing a child to sports, plenty of things can go wrong. Therefore, they know how critical it is for you to provide continued interest, support, guidance, and understanding, so that the child can *find* the fun and some of the benefits of youth sports can be achieved.

They know it isn't always easy.

But they know how much it mattered that *someone* in their lives raised his or own game in the name of better raising a child.

SECTION 1:
Why Sports Matter

"The Work of Children"

KARRIE WEBB was like a lot of four-year-olds, with the most innocent of ambitions: spend time with Grandma and Grandpa.

Her grandparents spent many Sundays on the course, playing nine holes. So, with her plastic club and plastic ball, she would tag along, getting in plenty of whacks and whiffs at the little white ball, unless she got exhausted.

"My grandfather would put me on his back or on the trolley and pull me around the rest of the way," Webb said.

It was never hard to drag her back out there, even though the game was slow, her improvement even slower.

"I enjoyed it," she said.

That's all that really mattered to her at the time.

That's all that would matter to any child of that age.

It wasn't necessary, or even possible, for Karrie to comprehend how much those experiences would matter to her future. They would have mattered even if her future did not include a prosperous and decorated career in the sport, culminating with a spot in the World Golf Hall of Fame. They would have mattered in the way that play of all kinds can matter for every child—as a vehicle for physical, mental, and emotional growth, the kind of vehicle that you should endorse for a child even if you don't have a strong passion for sports.

"Golf has shaped who I am as a person," Webb said.

That is a role that all sorts of play can often, well, play. The relationship is bidirectional: Children can shape play according to their age and stage of development, as well as their interests and talents. In turn, play can shape children in more ways than anyone can imagine.

Golf offered Karrie an outlet for physical engagement, staying in shape, releasing energy, and developing her fine (small muscle) and gross (large muscle) motor skills.

It offered her a platform to problem-solve and experiment, to learn about herself as she was learning about this vast new environment. She was learning about colors as she searched for the right tee from which to start. She was learning math through counting strokes and gauging distances. She was learning about distinctions and differences, and that, in this unique environment, smaller numbers were better than bigger numbers, shorter grass was preferable to taller grass, and sand was something to be avoided, not explored with a shovel. She was learning to remember and apply what others showed her, from grip to stance to swing.

Further, golf offered Karrie an arena for emotional evolution. That component of play is more complicated and can take more time to reveal itself, but it is no less critical. Play presents numerous opportunities for a child to discover how to communicate and, in a best-case scenario and with the guidance of a caring other, adequately manage feelings. Karrie was learning how to move on to the next shot without letting the last bad one linger. She was learning etiquette: how to wait her turn, respect others, and follow rules. She was learning to find her own fun.

She was being a kid, come what may—and plenty of good came from it.

Play, after all, comes naturally to children. They are hardwired to do it. As Donald Winnicott, the noted British psychoanalyst during the middle of the twentieth century, wrote: "Play is literally the work of children." Every child tells his or her own story through it in its most innocent form and stage.[3] Play is not really about victory. It is about discovery.

An infant's play begins passively through unspoken and spoken interactions with a caregiver, such as joyful gestures, exaggerated facial expressions, and soothing voice tones that engage the senses through imitation and repetition. The activity becomes more physically complex as a toddler enters early childhood, gaining greater awareness of bodily separateness, walking and then running on his or her own. It also becomes more mentally intricate, with the progression from peek-a-boo to hide-and-seek to Simon Says, requiring ever more advanced skills of thinking, memory, movement, language, and coordination. And it can become more emotionally intense, since it is human nature to get excited when things go your way and frustrated when they do not. Children can display these emotions through everything from shrieks to tears, from high-fives to clenched fists. Play not only forces children to learn how to acknowledge and deal with their feelings, but also gives adults an opportunity to assist them when they can do neither.

As these progressions occur, it is natural for a child to develop curiosity and then seek to expand his or her play space; it is also healthy so long as the child is under the protective umbrella of a watchful adult. On a playground or a backyard, on a grass field or a jungle gym, a child can find a sense of freedom and start to find him or herself through solitary, interactive, and even imaginary forms of unstructured play.

Simply, when play comes without value judgments and expectations, as it should for the young children participating in it, those children tend to find it enjoyable and rewarding, as Karrie did. And when something

---

3   D. W. Winnicott, *Playing and Reality* (New York, NY: Basic Books, 1971).

is enjoyable and rewarding, and especially if it is accompanied by adult reassurance, a child is more likely to continue and repeat the activity, as Karrie did. With repetition and practice, not only might improvement result, but the child will also feel a greater connection with his or her bodily movement and capability, as Karrie did.

So, yes, it's good to get your kids to play.

As much as possible.

"Even if you can't afford anything, just take him to the park," former NFL Pro Bowl cornerback **Patrick Surtain** said. "Let him experience little league sports in general, because all of us played it."

This sounds simple enough.

Yet there's no question there is a macro "play" problem in America, one prevalent enough that major professional sports organizations, such as the NFL and NBA, have started kid-centered activity programs such as Play 60 and NBA Fit, respectively, providing forums for participants to get in shape while, admittedly, reaping the additional benefit of creating a stronger connection to potential sports consumers. That problem is a result of sociological, familial, and financial norms and conditions in so many communities, and is something that you, as the adult, need to help address. There's a need for you to adjust to the times and still make play a priority in your own home and neighborhood.

"Outside Was the Thing"

LONG BEFORE he was "Too Tall" and a member of the Dallas Cowboys' famed "Doomsday Defense," **Ed Jones** was a kid on a farm in Jackson, Tennessee, a place blessed with fields aplenty.

That was the late 1950s.

Kids couldn't play video games. They couldn't search the Internet. They couldn't watch ESPN or MTV or pop in a DVD. They might not have even seen a television up close, let alone one or two or three or more in their homes.

Kids hardly needed to be pushed out the door to play.

They were anxious to join the kids playing already.

That's not what Jones sees anymore, even in intact families. Since so many parents are working, they can't always be home to encourage their children to, as he puts it, "go out and do things."

In the 1970s, when future NFL offensive lineman **Keith Sims** was growing up, parents tended to be home earlier and more often than they are now. Yes, the television was a presence, but his folks pushed him away from it. "We just played tackle football every day after school or baseball or something active," he said.

The same goes for future Major League pitcher **Jamie Moyer** during his youth in a small town outside of Philadelphia. "We could ride our bikes and play all day, come home for lunch or dinner, come home at dark," Moyer said. "We don't live in that kind of society anymore, unfortunately. It's pretty difficult to do that everywhere in our country."

All-pro NFL receiver **Reggie Wayne** remembers the 1980s the same way: "Outside was the thing. Everybody was outside, playing basketball, playing football."

Now?

There is a societal shift away from unstructured outdoor play, one that finds support in several studies, including one by the Stanford

University School of Medicine,[4] and in the observations of the athletes we interviewed.

"You see playgrounds empty," former NBA guard **Sam Cassell** said.

The former NBA star **Grant Hill** recalled "an age of innocence," when he would go to the cul-de-sac or playground where the kids would develop on their own, without supervision, through everything from hide-and-seek to kickball and eventually to more complex sports. "All those games, where there are not adults around, in a weird kind of way you're doing things, you're being athletic, you're having fun. And I think that kind of stuff plays a large part in kids developing and falling in love with sports."

That connection, however, is not a foremost concern to every school official and city planner. Inside schools and out in the community, kids are finding fewer places and times to run free. Instead they run into obstacles. Schools, under pressure to meet standardized testing requirements, have cut back recess to allocate more time for exam preparation.[5] Communities facing budget constraints and holding other priorities higher have failed to maintain their play spaces or to locate them in easily accessible areas. A recent study by the Centers for Disease Control and Prevention declared that there is "no safe and appealing place, in many communities, to play or be active," and that only one in five kids reside within a half-mile of a park or playground.

All of this, in the context of a world that is or merely seems less safe than it did, compels some parents to take the path of less resistance, keeping kids inside to make monitoring easier. Technology has exacerbated that trend, advancing to the point that kids, mimicking adults, also find that arrangement increasingly alluring. Many simply don't want to leave the

---

4   "Where the Playgrounds Are," *USA Weekend Magazine*, September 2–4, 2011.
5   "All school, no play," by Stephanie Pappas, Aug. 15, 2011, http://today.msnbc. msn.com/id/44123365/ns/today-parenting_and_family/t/all-school-no-play-kids-learning-suffers-without-recess-experts-say/#.UH8skpE_eYs

house because they don't want to leave the television, the video game console, or the computer, all of which hook them with constant sensory stimulation. Thus, that shift becomes one toward more sedentary and solitary activity.

"The PlayStations have taken over," Wayne said.

And the Xboxes. And the Wiis. And the iPads. And the smart phones. Soon it will be something else—maybe as soon as tomorrow.

This technological march has even changed what many children consider cool.

"Now if you are the best kid on the video game, you are the most popular kid in the school," future Hall of Fame running back **Edgerrin James** said. "Where it used to be if you were the best athlete."

Few of these pursuits on their own are inherently or entirely destructive. Some provide educational value; some require dexterity; some even involve interaction with another child or adult. It's only when kids participate in them obsessively and to the exclusion of physical exertion that the tradeoff becomes too costly. As **Orestes Destrade**, a former Major Leaguer who has covered the Little League World Series for ESPN, put it: "Our kids are growing up and getting more information and less play attention."

It shouldn't be surprising that so many are getting fat.

"It is really a bad situation now because kids are not in shape," record-setting Olympic long jumper **Bob Beamon** said. "Diabetes. Obesity is knocking on kids' doors."

Actually, it's already knocking many down. Nature can't be discounted for its role in obesity, with the trouble often starting in the DNA; genetics, family history, and even cultural background can all contribute. But you, as the caregiver, are not helpless. You can nurture a better outcome by setting the right example so kids don't develop destructive eating habits, and by probing for the deeper emotional issues that could be leading a kid to consistently turn to comforting sweets. You can keep a kid off the couch from time to time—or at least keep the bags of sugary and salty snacks away so reaching in and pigging out doesn't become the default activity.

You need to do this because the combination of sedentary lifestyles and supersized appetites is conspiring to drive some scary statistics, with obesity rates nearly tripling among children and more than tripling among adolescents over the past three decades.[6] It is enough of an epidemic that in 2009, First Lady Michelle Obama, shortly after her husband's inauguration as president, created the "Let's Move" campaign, advocating for more activity as well as better nutrition, including lower-calorie school lunches. Many athletes have made this a mission as well, most notably **Shannon Miller**, the most decorated gymnast in United States history and president of the Shannon Miller Foundation.

Why does obesity matter?

Obesity can create breathing problems such as asthma and sleep apnea; it can cause high blood pressure and high cholesterol, which are primary risk factors for cardiovascular disease; and it lead to the development of Type II diabetes mellitus.[7] All of this can prove costly not only to the child's quality of life but also to the family's finances. Obesity can set off other emotional and psychological difficulties as well. If an overweight kid is teased, bullied, or isolated by peers, it can have long-lasting impact on self-esteem. None of this is easily reversible—those overweight when young tend to become overweight adults, their symptoms and challenges only increasing over time.

"I think kids should have an appetite to sweat and get the heart pumping for health reasons," Beamon said. "We as parents need to get them into some kind of activity."

Edgerrin James agreed: the onus is on the adults. He grew up in Immokalee, Florida, where he and his friends didn't have much other

---

6   Centers for Disease Control and Prevention, Adolescent and School Health: Childhood Obesity Facts, http://www.cdc.gov/healthyyouth/obesity/facts.htm.

7   Centers for Disease Control and Prevention, Overweight and Obesity: Basics about Childhood Obesity, http://www.cdc.gov/obesity/childhood/basics.html.

than idle time for exercise in the sweltering heat. He surmised that "nowadays the kids don't *want* to be outside," with indoor activities abundant even in the most impoverished areas.

So what do you, as an adult, do?

"You have to take the video games away from them," James said. "Take the joystick, step on the joystick, lock the door; make sure they've got to be outside. Force them outside. Make them get out there in that hot sun and make them compete with their peers. That's the first thing you have to do."

The overriding thing?

Expose kids to as much physical activity as possible.

"Once they find it, they love it," Shannon Miller said.

That was her experience, anyway, after being introduced to running clubs in private and public schools and other organizations that serve children. "We did it in school, so it would be less of a barrier for parents," said Miller, who won sixteen combined World Championship and Olympic medals between 1991 and 1996. "We still had parents who were hesitant, saying, 'We don't know if Johnny should do this.' But the results were that the grades were better, and the kids were calmer at home. Some of whose who were having issues in class, they became leaders. They could cheer for other kids; they could be that voice."

Roughly three thousand children participated initially, spending thirty minutes or more at least twice per week running, skipping, or walking and earning rewards and praise at various milestones. As her mission statement says, "Anything works as long as they are moving forward under kid power."

Kid power with an adult boost.

"It doesn't have to be an organized sport or cost a lot of money," Miller said. Not if the adults are providing the right input and endorsing the right values.

"The most important thing is establishing a foundation for a love of activity," Miller said. "It's about a game of tag. But it's also about a family walk before dinner. It's about getting the family involved, not just the children, because the family buys the food. If you're a good role model, that will help you get your kids involved at a young age. If they're active at a young age, they are more likely to be more fit for the rest of life. And the inverse is true too."

In that way it can serve as a gateway to health. That construct applies to the concept of play as a whole.

Early play, as we described in this chapter, can serve as a healthy gateway to organized sports—provided, of course, that a child found that play enjoyable. The inverse of that is true as well. If a child doesn't enjoy play for play's sake in its most stripped-down, least-structured form, how can the child be expected to get excited for everything that's just around the developmental corner?

More fun can be found in organized sports. So can greater challenges.

"A Much Greater Purpose"

ORGANIZED SPORTS can be costly, complicated, and time-consuming. They require commitment, not just on the part of a child but on the part of an adult who gets involved. They may cause you, as that adult, to ponder the following as your child approaches the age of participation:

Why?

Why for your kid?

Why for you?

There isn't one answer, of course. There are lots of answers, and they differ depending on the circumstances.

This is one answer given:

"Sports keep kids out of trouble," NFL Pro Bowl running back **Maurice Jones-Drew** said.

They certainly can, for the hours that they occupy the child. They certainly can serve as a hobby and passion that focuses, challenges, and directs.

"Idle time is the devil's workshop," seven-time NBA All-Star **Alonzo Mourning** said. "So when kids get out of school, in between the times of three and seven or eight o'clock, if nobody is there between that time to tell them what they need to do, to show them that encouragement and support and put some structure and discipline in their lives, then they are going to fall by the wayside."

Leagues, teams, and coaches certainly can provide some of that encouragement, support, structure, and discipline. They can get kids through days and situations.

"There are so many professional athletes I talk to who say sports was a support system for them when going through a parent's divorce or a family having financial hardship," NFL kicker **Jay Feely** said. "That's what you want for your kids. You want sports to be something that helps you create discipline and hard work."

Certainly you do. Yet what is often overlooked is the way that devotion to sports can drive the child to develop discipline and embrace hard work in other places, such as the classroom. If a child comes to enjoy an athletic activity, you as the adult get a shot to receive the payoff. You can leverage that enjoyment. You can use the allure of continuing participation to insist upon a serious approach to other responsibilities, especially academic ones.

"To get a kid to do homework, and if he wants certain things, like new shoes for basketball, you can always dangle that carrot over him," ten-time NBA All-Star **Ray Allen** said. "So you can say 'Take care of school, and I'll help you.'"

Many of the athletes we interviewed heard something similar from adults during their own childhoods. Academic standards have been institutionalized at the highest levels of sports, such as high school and college. In youth sports, however, those standards must largely come from the home. Often they do.

Mary Joe Fernandez's carrot was the tennis court. Her parents' priority?

"Always school," she said. "That was what they cared about the most. They would let me miss school to go to events, but only if I kept a great average. It was good."

Even as she developed into a great player, their message was consistent:

The sport could not be everything. Balance was required. Fernandez still needed to study. She still needed to be a kid. "We would be driving to Orlando, and we would be halfway there, and my father would say, 'Would you rather play a tournament or go to Disneyworld?'" Fernandez recalled. "He would say, 'You know, we're going to Disneyworld.'"

At age fourteen, Mary Joe felt external and internal pressure to drop out of school, to turn pro, to stay on par with any of her peers anywhere in the world.

"My parents were like absolutely not," Fernandez said. "'You could get hurt. You need school to fall back on.'"

Leon Searcy already looked the part of an offensive lineman as a kid, but his mother, Erea, a schoolteacher, wouldn't let him play the part, not until he posted a B-plus average. He had to wait until his senior season to start knocking people around. "You can imagine being the biggest kid in high school and not playing. There was a lot of pressure on me. I thank her to this day. When I made it to the pros, it was easier for me."

Searcy would play eleven NFL seasons. One of his contemporaries was **Antonio Freeman**, who played ten after being raised much the same way. Freeman's parents "never allowed [him] to think it was all about sports." They made it clear what had to come first. That meant not only making Antonio do his assignments, but also making sure he didn't sprint through them just so he could sprint out to the field.

"You can be a great athlete, but if you are not a good scholar then you are not going to have a chance," said Freeman, a Pro Bowl selection and Super Bowl champion during a decade as an NFL receiver. "So many of the parents in today's society base so much on their child's talent. They need to be accountable to get an education. I say, stress to these kids to at least get a C average to play and, if something comes of sports, that's great."

Chris Bosh's mother and father stressed academics as much as basketball, even as the future Miami Heat star was growing into a dominant force. "They didn't want me to be this kid who just played basketball. I always had other interests and we built on that."

Education was stressed so much throughout **Andre Dawson's** childhood that when he would later try out for the Kansas City Royals as a high school senior, he was worried about how his grandmother would react if he were chosen. "I was one of three finalists," Dawson said. "I kind of tried to think about how I would address that with her. And it was scary, the thought of what her response was going to be." After all, his grandmother's message had always been: "Baseball is recreation. If you have God-given talent or ability, it will come out. There's another time for it."

It wasn't Dawson's time to turn pro, as it turned out, and he ended up getting his degree from Florida A&M University before embarking on a Hall of Fame professional career, one in which he earned as many plaudits for the way he conducted himself as the way he crushed baseballs.

So, sure, sports should be put in their proper place. That's quite different from suggesting they have *no* place in a child's development. **Bruce Bowen** certainly knew better when he was playing basketball at West Edison Fresno High in California. The son of parents who both struggled with addiction, Bowen knew not only that he needed to be on top of school to stay in sports, but also that sports could keep him in school. He could use sports to further his education. At a time prior to caller ID, he called college coaches and disguised his voice, telling them "to check out this kid." He received a scholarship to Cal-State Fullerton and became a three-time NBA champion.

Feely certainly knows better as well.

"Sports can be really transformational in somebody's life," Feely said. "In a lot of instances, it can be life-saving."

Sports can cross borders, transcend cultures, and give children hope just about anywhere. Consider Feely's partnership with the Mission of Hope in the impoverished, earthquake-ravaged country of Haiti, where there are more than a million orphans. Not much has been done to make their daily lives better, especially since the CNN cameras left. Not much makes them run toward something with broad smiles on their faces.

"But you bring a soccer ball out, and they are drawn to it," Feely said. "They come out of the woodwork. It's using sports as a lure to draw kids in."

It's using sports as a carrot, the same way so many American parents can and do.

"They're not only nourished mentally, but they get breakfast and lunch," Feely said. "You're providing a goal, a dream, and an educational foundation. It's such a great example of where you can use sports for something that has a much greater purpose."

The story of **Torii Hunter** is another powerful example.

"I used sports to make my life," Hunter said.

His life didn't look promising early on. His surroundings were squalor, his bed often no more than a towel draped over a hard floor. His father, Theotis, was an electric engineer but also a crack addict, and often absentee. His mother, Shirley, was a teacher—caring and supportive yet overburdened with four children to feed. His older brother Tyru had the best intentions, even if he didn't introduce Torii to the best role models. Tyru was a gang member and close friends with other gang members who, by extension, would also become Torii's friends.

"But he wouldn't let me join," Hunter said. "And they all were scared to do anything. He protected me; his name kind of protected me. 'That's Tyru's brother, leave him alone.'"

When left alone, Torii played. He played typical kids' games, and then he played baseball and basketball and football. He played for the reason that all young children play, wherever they are, whatever their situation and surroundings. He played for fun and freedom. It was only when he got older and came to understand more about his circumstances that he played with purpose. He began to play not merely as an escape from his reality but as a means to forge a better one.

"Everything that we went through, it kind of motivated me and pushed me really hard to make it," Hunter said. "I always told myself, 'I've got to get out of here. I've got to do this.'"

Through organized sports, Hunter got to do things and go places he had never imagined. When he was thirteen, he won a state baseball tournament and advanced to a regional in Santa Fe, New Mexico. He stayed with a host family for a month.

"They dined together," Hunter said. "They dined *together*. They hung out on Sundays and bowled. We got up in the morning and ate breakfast together. I was like, 'What the hell? Eating breakfast?' Me, as a kid from the ghetto, I had never been outside my environment. I couldn't afford to go nowhere else; this was the only thing I knew, this society. So I left and went to another environment, and I was like, 'Man, this is perfect. This is what I want for my family.' So it pushed me. It pushed me to broaden my horizons, to go out and get a scholarship, because I knew my parents couldn't afford the tuition."

So, yes, he has wondered...

What if he hadn't uncovered and built upon his God-given ability?

What if he hadn't had sports?

"It probably would have been a different route for me," said Hunter, who signed a two-year, $26 million contract with Detroit during the 2012 offseason.

You might view Torii Hunter as an extreme example. Undeniably, he was in some ways, for worse and for better.

Not every child has the misfortune of growing up, as Hunter did, in a place like Pine Bluff, Arkansas, consistently ranked among America's five most impoverished cities. Not every child confronts quite the same degree of familial dysfunction. When probed by *USA Today* in 2005, Hunter could recall only one positive childhood memory with his father, a fishing trip at age nine, compared to so many traumatic ones, including the time that a crack pipe fell out of his Bulls jacket, the one his father had borrowed, when he raised his hand in class. Not every child is blessed with the awareness and discipline to recognize, and then execute, an exit strategy from such a seemingly dead-end situation, even though many have used sports that way.

"How many kids live in the slums and ghettos?" former NFL safety **Bennie Blades** said. "How can they get out? They have to have an avenue to get out. Fortunately for us, the avenue was sports."

Not every child is endowed with the athletic talent to get out, of course, the talent that allowed Hunter to star in three sports other than baseball in high school before blossoming into a four-time Major League Baseball All-Star outfielder.

Not many American children are as challenged as Torii Hunter, and not every child needs such a heaping helping of hope. However, every child has a chance to take something meaningful from unstructured play and an organized youth sports experience.

In the words of Ray Allen, words seconded by so many elite athletes: "There's so many lessons you learn that are sport-oriented that end up being life lessons."

"By playing team sports, you learn accountability, how to be accountable not only for yourself but to your teammates," said retired quarterback **Chad Pennington**, the two-time NFL Comeback Player of the Year, a son of a Physical Education teacher and the father of three sons. "You also learn how to come under authority, whether you agree with it or disagree with it, and learn how to work with that authority. You learn the team concept, you learn dedication and hard work, all those core values that are essential to any type of success in life, whether it is business or family or whatever. You learn those things through athletics. No matter what level you play on, they never change. They always stay the same."

Over more than four decades ago in 1970, John Dockery approached his star Jets teammate **Joe Namath** with an idea.

"He asked if I would be interested in starting a camp to use football to teach kids about life," Namath recalled.

More than four decades later, the camp still continues with the same goals in mind.

"Football has so many things you can learn from," Namath said. "Getting knocked down, coming back, owning up to responsibility, counting on one another. There are so many life lessons that you may not get otherwise. And learning not to be so thin-skinned maybe. Learning to take care of your instrument."

The instrument for the athlete is the body.

The instruction for the child goes beyond it.

"We use football to teach kids about life," Namath said proudly.

You can use virtually any sport this way with a child, whether it is baseball or basketball or soccer, or even the so-called individual endeavors like tennis, golf, or gymnastics. All can be effective in cultivating a child's growth, provided that the child has the proper guidance and the patience and desire to accept that counsel.

"As they get older, they've got coaches, they've got friends, they've got other friends' parents," Ray Allen said. "That are *all* helping them grow."

The growth comes from exposure to all the lessons that Pennington so perfectly listed. Over time, sports can teach kids the rules and the importance of respecting those who implement and enforce them. They can teach kids enduring values, not in theory but through practice and experience, such as sportsmanship, unity, accountability, resourcefulness, and resilience.

"About Being Fair"

FREEDOM IS one of the attractions of unstructured, unsupervised play.

In the backyard, driveway, or alley, kids are free to make their own rules and then bend them any way that the group decides. They can set their own out-of-bounds line: the tree or the mailbox or the neighbor's garbage can. They can choose their own sides and decide how many players should participate at once. They can choose never to call a foul or penalty, no matter how rough the contact. They can play without a clock, the buzzer sounding when someone's mom screams that it's time to finally finish some homework.

As stated earlier, that sort of play has considerable value for exercise, socialization, skill development, confidence, and mostly, fun and freedom.

Organized sports, however, represent the next healthy step.

This is because, as every child must learn, life has rules. Those rules help provide order, structure, and safety. Growing up, a child comes to know the rules of his or her particular house and classroom and the consequences of failing to follow any of those.

In this same vein, organized sports have some fairly universal truths:

No hands in soccer.

No feet in basketball.

No more than three strikes in baseball.

No more than four downs in football.

Every sport has its own set of requirements, restrictions, and equipment. Fields of play have generally accepted shapes, boundaries, sizes, and surfaces.

Even in a society obsessed with winning, there's an understanding that if the rules are not followed, the result isn't fair and won't count. It's not okay to simply make rules up. A baseball runner can't decide, after getting tagged out, to just take the next base anyway. A basketball player can't decide to just scoop up the ball and carry it to the hoop because it's easier than dribbling. A football player can't run out of bounds to escape a tackle, sprint back onto the field, and score a touchdown.

To participate in either a team or individual sport, one must find a way to conform to these established rules. One must come to understand that they take precedence over the desire for victory because they are in place to keep the playing field fair.

One must be what we commonly call a "good sport," one who exercises good sportsmanship.

There's nothing inherently wrong with competition, after all, even for a developing child. For former tennis star Mary Joe Fernandez, competition provided propulsion as well as preparation: "Life is competitive; you can't avoid it. Whether at school, trying to get good grades, or trying to get a job, you are going to face competition one way or another."

When she was eight or nine, Fernandez became obsessed with the little yellow ball, slamming it against her bedroom wall, against her family's refrigerator, and ultimately, all over a court. As she started playing tournaments, she learned about playing fair even as she strove to win. She learned to use her brain: "I was never a big hitter, so I had to work on strategy, how to work a point. Just like in life, you have different methods of approaching situations. You have to figure it out."

She learned how to deal with her emotions when her plan worked and when it didn't.

These days, in addition to her role as a broadcaster, Fernandez is a mother to a girl and boy, both close to the age when she started playing tennis. She sees plenty of kids who don't handle results well, who are cocky when they win and will do anything to keep from losing—and plenty of parents and coaches who encourage this behavior.

"The cheating ... I am shocked at how parents don't stop their kids from cheating," Fernandez said. "Cheating has been going on forever, and I just don't understand how that is okay. Obviously, temper tantrums and bad attitudes, they are hard, because that could be just the personality of the kid. But what are you teaching your child, the end justifies the means?"

Still, in spite of these irritations, she has no intentions to pull her kids out. She just won't tolerate the extremes. That means no gloating; if they win, congratulate the opponent and move on. That means no cheating; if they lose, just learn from it.

"I always tell my kids that cheaters don't make it in life," Fernandez said. "My daughter has had a couple of instances where there's been blatant cheating. Some parents are like, 'Tell her to cheat back.' I go the other way. If [the opponent's shot] is anywhere near the line, even if it is out, you are going to call it good."

Above all?

"It's about being fair," she said. "You try to teach your child the right message. It is a sport, it is a game; you try to do your best, but mostly, behave your best."

By the time a child enters youth sports, he or she has likely heard the stern warning about cheating over and over, at home, at school, at a neighbor's house, or at a place of worship. Even so, cutting corners can be difficult to resist.

A child has many reasons for cheating. Some kids cheat thinking they will gain the attention, approval, or admiration of others, whether peers or outsiders, that they may not be getting otherwise. Some kids cheat simply not to be labeled as losers. Some kids cheat because they don't trust their skills and believe they have no other way to succeed. In the course of cheating, many children think little about getting caught, and even less about their conscience telling them an action is wrong. As they come to consistently rationalize their own behavior, that can serve to compromise their moral development, and they can lose a sense of self. It can also serve to impede their socialization, as the cheat is exposed, labeled, and perhaps shunned.

Karrie Webb has young nieces who are old enough to play board games, including Chutes and Ladders. "They don't like it when they have to go down the chute," the golfer said. "They want to cheat. Watching kids at that age, you're like, 'How do they know that?' But it's just human nature."

It is. The temptation to cheat is present in every activity, from a board game based solely on luck to an athletic endeavor which requires some skill to other enterprises in society. Yet one of the more redeeming elements of sports is that they are governed by the idea that there will be rules, and those not following those rules will be penalized or, perhaps, ejected, suspended, or banned. Children can get great value out of participation in athletic programs that put a premium on the respect for those rules, especially if the parents stress the importance of respecting those who teach, implement, and enforce them.

But there are also unwritten rules in sports that are equally important for every child to understand. One of those rules is that anyone giving a sport a try should give it their all.

"Being Committed"

BRUCE SMITH didn't kid about commitment.

Even as a kid.

"I've always said this," said Smith, a Hall of Fame defensive end. "I'd rather have my worst enemy playing alongside me, making the same sacrifices and being committed to the job at hand, than my best friend cutting corners he shouldn't be cutting."

Commitment is one of sports' core virtues; the expectation that an athlete will show dedication to the game and teammates. At a young age, a child may not have complete control over showing up on time. However, the child can show commitment in the way he or she shows respect to coaches and teammates, accepts a role or position, and above all, exhibits the effort and persistence required to successfully complete a task. What is unique about sports-related tasks for young children is that they combine elements of work and play.

"The thing I liked about organized sports for my kids was the discipline they had to learn to develop," said Hall of Fame receiver **Steve Largent**, a former US congressman from Oklahoma. "And that to me is the real benefit to getting involved in sports as they grow up."

These are necessary attributes in life. As **James McKnight** has found in his post-NFL career, companies are always asking these questions when considering candidates: "Can he or she take this task and complete it? Do they have an inner drive? Are they self-motivated or do they have to be pushed? Most athletes don't have to be motivated. They see the task, they perform the task, and they do everything to complete the task."

The question is whether the drive comes first or is developed through sports. And, as with the query about the chicken or the egg, it can't always be answered unequivocally. Many of the athletes we interviewed spoke matter-of-factly of possessing discipline and determination at a very early age. Many couldn't remember, in fact, when they didn't possess inner drive, the self-directed desire to accomplish something.

When growing up in Haiti, current NBA center **Samuel Dalembert** didn't want to be given the answer in class. "I would sit down for two hours and figure it out until I got it. Some friends would say to me, 'Man, it took you two hours to figure out the answer,' but at least I got it. That's the kind of person I was. That sort of thing would carry on to the field."

At that time, Dalembert knew nothing of basketball. He played soccer with kids twice his age and much more muscular. "I knew that I was going to get beat up, but I was still out there. I would never stand back. I was always the kind of guy joking around, be the smiling Sam, cracking jokes. I had that tenacity about me. I would go after something."

While Dalembert showed equal determination whether engaged in scholastic or athletic activity, many kids tend to put more of their time and energy into the latter. That's because they find sports more enjoyable than other things they could be doing.

Charles Johnson threw tennis balls against the wall to catch and block them, not because his father, Charles Jr., was pushing him to become a baseball catcher or any type of baseball player at all. He did it simply because he liked to. "I learned how to play the game by myself," said Johnson, a former Major League All-Star. He learned to work the game, love the game.

It was the same with Karrie Webb and golf.

"Ninety-five of the push came from myself," Webb said.

It was the same for **Santana Moss** with football.

"I just had the desire and passion for it," the long-time Washington Redskins receiver said. "I always wanted to do it."

Kids may not always realize that in doing something simply because they enjoy it they may be doing something else. They may be developing discipline, resilience, and ambition—which again are characteristics that every parent should hope to see sprout in a child.

Sanya Richards-Ross didn't start running in Jamaica because she believed it would lead her to four Olympic medals. "I did it for fun," Richards said. "Then I realized I was really good at it."

She realized that when at age seven she ran a faster mile than girls two years older; it was reinforced when she started winning championships in her age group.

"I wanted to train and get better," Richards-Ross said.

Jason Taylor didn't know that his early athletic play in Pennsylvania would put him on a path to enshrinement in Canton, Ohio. "I always had the fire burning inside to push myself and be the best," Taylor said. "Sometimes I frustrate myself, and that can be detrimental to me, but that is the way I've always been. At the end of the day, you have to have it inside of you. If you don't have it inside of you, then no one can push you further than you push yourself."

Sam Madison wasn't aware that, while trying to overcome a modest genetic obstacle, he was setting himself up for a long, lucrative NFL career as a cornerback, much of it on Taylor's side with the Dolphins and even on the AFC Pro Bowl squad. "The thing that worked for me was that I was always a small guy," Madison said. "Being that I worked harder, it gave me an edge. I always wanted to win. I always wanted to be the best."

Shannon Miller discovered this too. She found her sister's sport, gymnastics, particularly appealing because it combined fun and competition.

"It gave me a goal," Miller said. "You were going to be judged on that routine."

Gymnastics gave Miller a platform for accountability to herself. If she was not satisfied with the score, she was intrinsically motivated to work harder to achieve a better one.

All sports, even the individual ones, encourage dedication and effort in another way as well: through extrinsic motivation. That is the desire to please others, to earn recognition and approval, or even to receive some tangible reward like a trophy so you feel like you are doing your part.

Walt Frazier's fuel from childhood through a Hall of Fame NBA career was "the respect you gain from guys when you're good. When you give 100 percent and guys beat you, you can accept it. But then you also know if you keep working, you can attain that level."

Outsiders' views also influenced Madison. "I always wanted everyone to look up to me as a leader, to put the burden on my shoulders no matter what sport it was, and be somebody the guys wanted to follow."

He kept working, because he didn't want to let anyone down—not himself or anyone else. That's how sports motivate many kids. Kids don't want to let down their coaches, parents, grandparents … or peers.

"If you miss practice, you are letting the team down," former NFL All-Pro defensive end **Trace Armstrong** said. "If you decide to give lackadaisical effort, you are betraying the trust of the team. It is important for young kids to hear that. Kids have to understand that when they break that trust, that is serious."

Armstrong took it seriously from youth sports all the way through the pros. The point was best illustrated for him when he was in college. If one of his Arizona State teammates missed study hall or was late for practice and other players didn't know why, his coach John Cooper would discipline the entire team. "That was a great lesson," Armstrong said. "You better believe that ten minutes before the start of a team meeting, you would have ten guys working the payphones and trying to find out where he is."

The same accountability expectation applies in the so-called individual sports such as gymnastics, track, and tennis. Shannon Miller, Sanya Richards-Ross, and Mary Joe Fernandez all eventually competed in a group capacity at the highest levels, with Richards-Ross winning a gold medal in the relay at the 2008 Olympics and then another gold in the four-hundred-meter sprint in the 2012 Olympics, Miller's "Magnificent Seven" team winning a gold medal at the 1996 Olympics, and Fernandez winning two Grand Slam championships and two Olympic gold medals (1992, 1996) in doubles competition.

Many outside these athletes' circles may have perceived them to be on their own in competition.

In reality, they never were.

Others were counting on their commitment, whether in competition or practice.

"An individual sport is never done individually," speed skater **Jennifer Rodriguez** said. "There's not one person who can do it by themselves. There are a lot of people working to make you the best you can be."

"You know that the best thing you can do for your team is get the highest score individually that you can, since it doesn't do anyone standing on sidelines any good if you fall the first time," Miller said. "And I do feel like there is a team aspect in your gym, those girls you are working with day in and day out. They are the ones you live and breathe with."

Those are the ones that can help to make athletes better, and vice versa.

"A Bonding Force"

ELTON BRAND'S son, Elton Peace, was the typical toddler.

He had desires and demands.

"Everything is mine, mine, gimme, gimme, it's mine," Brand said.

That's normal and natural. Kids that age simply don't share. That's one reason why Brand planned to share the youth sports experience with his child, as soon as he could.

"When he's playing sports, he's going to learn he's on a team and he needs to share and care for another person," said Brand, a veteran NBA player. "In a team sport, you learn this is your friend, this is your buddy. We might be overmatched today, but we are going down with each other. You learn at that an early age."

As explained earlier, kids first learn to play by observing and imitating, and also through the guidance of an adult—the parent, for instance, rolling a ball to them. The next step for children is the realization that they can play *with* someone else in parallel and complementary fashion. That awareness of the other participant, as both friend and foe, can give rise to competition. When kids go from unstructured play to structured sports, that instinct to compete only intensifies. It occurs internally, with a child wanting to do his or her best and earn praise from an adult, whether a parent or coach. It occurs within the confines of the team when vying for the coach's attention or individual recognition or battling for a particular position or role, like a goalie, a quarterback, or the first spot in the batting order.

Team sports help to channel this competitive instinct because there's always a greater goal in mind: competing against the other team.

To do that effectively, it is necessary to cooperate. It is necessary to cooperate not only with friends, whose presence on the team might have convinced a child to sign up initially, but also with those a child may have never met prior to the first day of practice, those who may have their own cliques of friends on the team already. It is necessary to cooperate even if all the child has in common with a teammate is the team itself.

Former Major Leaguer Orestes Destrade, a broadcaster on ESPN's Little League World Series coverage from 2007–2009, believes that teamwork is such an ingrained expectation in sports that when he speaks to kids in schools, he uses an analogy: think of the teacher like a coach and classmates as teammates and work together on a project the way you would work to win. Think of the words that are used in business, and so many other aspects of society, to describe someone who puts the good of the group over his or her own personal aspirations: team player.

That phrase? Straight from sports.

And what is a team exactly? It is a collection of disparate parts. People are mixed together from different circumstances, at different developmental levels, and with different innate abilities, interest, and temperaments—and then expected to make each other better. This can be combustible, especially on the youth sports level where teams also become extracurricular social groups. They practice several times per week together. Carpools. Bus rides. Pizza parties. Sleepovers. Wins. Losses. Teams spend so much time together that when basketball star Walt Frazier turned pro, one of his toughest transitions was adapting to all the free time that teammates spent apart. Back in the good old days of youth sports, Frazier recalled, "We did *everything* as a team."

Some teams run into trouble. Some situations strain developing relationships. Not everyone gets along, and certainly not all the time.

Still, none of that sways **Chipper Jones**, the retired seven-time Major League All-Star, from this view:

"Team sports, there's nothing better."

There's nothing that better creates the conditions for learning and appreciating the principles of acceptance, patience, and sacrifice. There's nothing that offers quite the same opportunity to find common ground and a common cause with those not exactly alike.

"You can take so many different people from so many different backgrounds," Jones said. "And once you put the same uniform on and you go into battle, and you immerse yourself in the battle and you come out on top, having leaned on one of your teammates or having them lean on you, that's a bonding force that most times can't be broken."

The Braves' star isn't expecting any of his children to make careers of sports. Nevertheless he believes the exposure to team sports is helping them find their own places while making them more open-minded, well-rounded people.

As it did for him.

"You try to put them into situations where they have to interact with other kids, white, black, Hispanic, whatever," Jones said. "My main concern is that I want to make sure they are socially right, that they have every opportunity. We are not guarding them; we are not secluding them from everyone else."

Regardless of athletic talent, all kids can benefit from the forced socialization of sports. They can benefit from shared associations and common goals. They can benefit from hearing over and over that the only colors that should matter to teammates are the ones they share on their uniforms. They can benefit from hearing over and over the commitment these connections entail.

"You are always going to have personality conflicts, but the fact of the matter is, baseball is something that brings everybody together. It doesn't matter what color you are, what race, what ethnicity, what religion; you all go out there and play as a unit," Jones said. "You would be surprised how many personality conflicts or racial conflicts or whatever can all be resolved by going out there and creating that bond on the baseball field."

Organized sports helped **Shane Battier** resolve his internal conflicts with race. As a kid in Birmingham, Michigan, Battier didn't feel he fit anywhere. Raised by a black father and white mother in a mostly white neighborhood and entirely white elementary school, Battier often felt excluded, isolated, and misunderstood. In most settings, including the classroom, peers didn't really know what to make of him.

"But I had sports," Battier said.

Team sports.

Places where he could make others accept him.

The field. The court.

"Because I could kick a ball further than anyone else who could kick a ball, and because I was fast, I was always the first picked for baseball and basketball," Battier said. "You feel part of a group as a kid. As a kid, that's all you want. Sports are the great equalizer."

When guided by responsible adults, teams can be great multipliers, helping a child grow in a myriad of ways.

The chance to practice selflessness and sacrifice is among the reasons why former NFL Rookie of the Year **Troy Stradford** said, "If your kid isn't in sports, I believe they lack something."

They may miss the chance to learn from leaders.

"Learn to Be Coachable"

THESE DAYS countless people call Pat Riley "Coach." It is the ultimate term of reverence, and one that Riley has used for many others over the course of his life. He respected their authority on his way to becoming an authority figure himself. During a summer 2011 speech at the Miami Dolphins Touchdown Club, Riley—who had won a total of six NBA champions as either a player or coach and would soon win two more (2012, 2013) as a Miami Heat executive—referenced a book called *Iron John*, which was about the importance not only of fathers for sons but also of other male mentors for those sons.

"My father was a baseball player and a coach in the minor leagues for twenty years; he never made it to the big leagues," Riley told the audience. "But during that time, as my father but also as my coach, he was a man that introduced me to a lot of other people who became mentors. I had a father as a coach, but I have had sixteen coaches in my life who were all mentors to me."

He said they were people he could turn to and who would listen to him, since father–son relationships aren't copasetic all the time.

"They become wars," Riley said. "One of the greatest things about being an athlete, about being in sports, is that I was born in a coaching background and I lived in the philosophy of what coaches believe. Each of the coaches I played for had something incredibly special for me."

Coaches at youth levels have had this effect on countless kids and teens across the country.

"Coaches spend just as much time with the kids as the parents do," said **Henri Crockett**, who played linebacker in the NFL for seven seasons while his brother Zack played fullback for thirteen. "Moms are going to be moms. But it's that coach, that outside influence, that you as a kid don't want to let down. You are going to look to them a lot for guidance, sometimes even before you tell your Mom. You might talk to your coach more than your parents."

This possibility might make some parents and primary caregivers uncomfortable. And, yes, there are appropriate limits to everything. Yet on the whole, exposure to constructive authority figures should be welcomed, and a child's receptivity to those figures should be embraced. Respect for such authority is one of the most valuable things a child can take from the sports experience, with the expectation that participants take in the teachings of those with greater knowledge and experience, not just for their own good but for the good of the group. You should view those valuable voices as extensions of your own, imparting and reinforcing positive values but simply in a sports context. Take heart in a child's earnest attempts to process, access, and start adopting those precepts.

You should view your role as complementary not adversarial. You should allow the coach some latitude to challenge, so long as he or she also lifts.

"Coaching and parenting, it's very, very similar," said **Allan Houston,** a former NBA All-Star and current New York Knicks executive, a father of seven, and the 2007 Father of the Year by the National Fatherhood Initiative for work that has included father–son and father–daughter basketball retreats throughout New York City's five boroughs. "You praise them, and you correct them. You find that balance."

For Houston's father, Wade, coaching and parenting were exactly the same, especially when Houston enrolled to play for him in 1989 at the University of Tennessee. Before that Houston had plenty of other adults enabling and accelerating his athletic progress with his dad's endorsement.

"I just think the one common denominator that I've seen in coaching and parenting that always works ... kids, athletes, they want to expect a certain standard, and that is consistency," Houston said. "So a kid, he may not like you at first, but if you say that 'we are going to practice this time every day' or 'you are going to get up at this time every day' or 'you are going to do your homework at this time every day,' they may not admit it, but that works and they like it. It is effective and they respond to it better."

Consistency and confidence.

"They also have to know that you know what you're doing," Houston said. "Otherwise, they see through it, that you don't know what you're doing."

Like parents who expect the completion of homework and chores, sometimes coaches need to be stern and show tough love in order to get a message across and achieve a desired result. **Jon Ogden**, who didn't start playing football until seventh grade and eventually made the Pro Football Hall of Fame, thinks that all of his coaches, even the strictest ones, "were looking out for my best interests," and that coaches in general "are hard on you for your own good. You've got to believe that with coaches, they're not out to be hard-asses *just* to be that way. If he tells you to do it like this, do it like this. They're out there to make you a better person, a better player."

Sometimes coaches need to delay a youth athlete's gratification and make that athlete work for it, the way that Carol City High football coach Walt Frazier kept Santana Moss hungry. "He didn't give me the ball until he felt it was time. That really humbled me so much," Moss said.

With coaches as well as parents, it can sometimes take years for a child to fully appreciate the purpose and intent of such coaching or management techniques. This is the case in all aspects of life when someone who has mastered an activity is imparting that knowledge to someone less experienced. Way back when, Walt Frazier—the former New York Knicks star, not Moss's coach—didn't appreciate the inflexible manner in which his uncle taught him to drive. "He'd go, 'What did that sign say, it says stop! So why in the hell didn't you stop?' So he was very strict, but I am a good driver."

The Crocketts' coaches were very strict when it came to behavior and performance. But the brothers both benefited, as people and players. "To this day we thank them for being tough on us," Henri Crockett said.

Youth and prep coaching can be a thankless job at times, and hardly a lucrative one. Many on the youth levels work as volunteers. Even on the high school level, the compensation invariably isn't commensurate with the required commitment. For most, coaching is a labor of love, and that love is sometimes unrequited.

"Kids don't understand that these coaches, these teachers, these counselors are giving up their time, their patience, their body to try to help you out," said **Tim Hardaway**, a former NBA All-Star. "It may seem like it's negativity because we want you to work on your game, we want you to excel, we see the potential in you. These kids nowadays are taking it to a new level when they think it's negativity, but it's not. They need to listen and understand that it's constructive criticism."

"You *learn* to be coachable," Olympic speed skater Jennifer Rodriguez said. "Not everyone is coachable, but if you want to be one of the best, you have to learn to take criticism."

Crockett believes some parents need to learn something else: to let go, especially when it is clear that a coach "stands for something, great character, great disciplinarian." That, of course, is not always easy. It is human nature for you, as a parent, to be overprotective and to rally to a child's defense in nearly every situation. Yet that it is not necessarily a constructive reaction. It is impossible for a coach who is trying to lead and teach to do either effectively, with overbearing adults constantly sending mixed messages to the child, criticizing the coach's every decision and undermining his or her voice.

Sam Cassell was known as a free spirit, fast talker, and pugnacious personality during his fifteen seasons playing in the NBA. But what happened when his son was rising through the basketball ranks? "I never once questioned the coach's game plan," said Cassell, who is now an NBA assistant coach with the Washington Wizards. "Not once."

It's essential for you to establish with a child that, in the sports environment—whether on the field, court, or bus—the coach is in charge. Even if you might not set or enforce a guideline the same way a coach does, that doesn't mean the coach's instruction is inappropriate. For instance, just because you might clean up regularly after a child at home, it doesn't make it wrong when the coach orders extra laps when the child leaves his or her equipment lying around. When you are with your child, you should reinforce the legitimacy of the coach's constructive teachings. When you are with the coach, you should avoid confrontation that will cause the child to question the coach's legitimacy.

"A lot of times parents don't want coaches to yell at the kids," Crockett said. "I would say, 'Let the coach do what he has to do to get through to that kid.' You want that. And that's what parents don't understand. The parents look at it like, 'They're hurting my child.' But a kid looks at it later like, 'Thank you for making me the person I am today.' Don't look at it like, 'Who is coaching my kid?' Look at it like, 'Who is raising my kid?'"

Of course, if you look at it in such stark terms, then it is also necessary to closely examine each individual situation. Not all authority, after all, is worthy of unequivocal trust and respect. Even if every coach has the purest of intentions, that doesn't mean that all come to the job with the

same training and experience, especially in the a꜡
It's not sufficient to drop or ship off your kid an⠀
this book's final section, we will take you throu⠀
and the actions to consider.

But sometimes you just need to step up like
grandson Jay would occasionally whine about a
had been a basketball coach himself.

"He'd pull me aside and set me straight," Jay Feely said.

The message?

"It is your job to overcome whatever obstacle gets in your way."

"It's about the Inconvenience"

DAVID ECKSTEIN started as a second baseman. He preferred to be
a shortstop. So he worked tirelessly at his fielding and, in spite of his
modest stature, improved steadily, steadily enough to expect to continue
playing the glamour position.

Then David encountered the youth sports equivalent of a bad hop,
a circumstance completely beyond his control: the coach who favors his
kin.

"He wanted his kid to play shortstop, so that was the end of my
playing shortstop," Eckstein said.

He was hardly the first, only, or last kid to bump up against such
bias.

"There were times when I was frustrated as a young kid," said Charles
Johnson, the former All-Star catcher. "When you play in a younger league,

coaches play politics with kids. Since they are coaching, they
eir son. Kids say I know I am a way better [player] than that guy,
d I see kids quit."

Charles didn't quit, and neither did David. The latter just kept
squirming his way into a new spot.

"Then I played third base, second base, to the outfield," Eckstein
said.

Once he enrolled at Sanford High in Florida, that versatility was of
value, especially since that former Little League coach had taken over
the high school team. By then David was most adept at centerfield, but
he still took over at second base and never looked back. In retrospect, his
early removal from shortstop, however unjustified, helped him—not just
for that period but for a much later one.

"It saved my arm," Eckstein said, noting the strain of throwing
regularly across the infield.

He would need that arm for his appearances in two Major League
All-Star games, for his starts at shortstop—yes, shortstop—in two
World Series, and even for the lifting of the 2006 World Series MVP
trophy. The coach's son, meanwhile, maxed out at the college level.

"The coach will tell you his son was two or three inches taller, had
a bigger wing span, and could pick it in the hole," Eckstein said smiling.
"Yet neither of us could throw it across the diamond."

David proved to be a diamond in the rough, sparkling brighter as
a result of the early adversity he encountered. Sports, like little else in
modern society, allow participants an opportunity to adjust, respond,
persevere, and overcome in split-seconds and over the long term, and in
every imaginable sort of situation. Sports gave David the opportunity to
test and then strengthen his resilience and resourcefulness. Faced with a
challenge, he proved to others and to himself that he was able to adapt,
bend without breaking, and keep finding ways to stay in. He didn't take
the easy way out.

It's natural for a kid to feel overwhelmed by uncontrollable occurrences or furious about unfair decisions and events. It's human to hurt after losses and feel small and sad after individual failure, wondering if anyone else has ever played so poorly before or been such a disappointment to so many. Still, there should be some comfort in the knowledge that just about every type of adversity has been experienced by someone before, including many athletes a youth may greatly admire. Kids may assume that for those athletes everything came easy. That's simply not the case. As we will reveal the chapter "You Have to Have Failure," many of those athletes look back at their childhood sports obstacles and setbacks, even the most upsetting at the time, in appreciation rather than in anger. They believe that a trial, whether it originated externally or internally, made them tougher and better and played a role in their later success. The adult should take comfort in that knowledge as well, that nothing a child goes through is entirely unusual, and doesn't necessarily make a positive youth sports experience unattainable.

What if a child isn't among the coach's favorites, perhaps for reasons unknown or unfair?

Dwight Howard, even with his enormous ability, dealt with this issue.

"I've been put in different types of situations where I was the best player on the team, but the coach didn't like me, so he did not play me," Howard said.

The coach might regret that in retrospect. Howard, now with the Rockets, is arguably the NBA's most dominant active center.

James McKnight went through something like this as well, and more than once.

Asthma was enough of an obstacle for McKnight. However, he also had a middle school track coach who, as was the case for many in the 1980s, didn't understand the condition—and in turn, didn't understand him. When McKnight tired easily, the coach mistook it for laziness rather than a symptom of his disease. "He tried everything he could to run me off the team," McKnight said. "I had an inner drive, so I kept fighting it."

At Apopka High in Florida, McKnight battled another coach who was unsympathetic to his circumstances. McKnight had been raised a Seventh-Day Adventist, which meant no work or play from sundown Friday through sundown Saturday. Consequently, he needed to skip football practice for church on Saturday mornings. The coach kept McKnight on junior varsity through eleventh grade and told the coaches of that team to avoid playing him. Those coaches let him play anyway, and as a high school senior, McKnight finally got a break: a varsity receiver quit. He was needed.

"I had a good season, played well in college, graduated, went to the NFL, and [the high school coach] tried to take credit for coaching me in high school," McKnight said. "I didn't rub it in his face. I came back to the school because it was about the kids. I wasn't holding a grudge, but his negativity made me work even harder. At the time [I was in school], I was searching for his approval. By the end of the day, I was going to be the best I could be. He may not like me, I thought, but nothing was going to stop me. A lot of kids are not that strong."

That may be true. Yet so is this: without enduring something difficult or painful, many kids can't truly know the extent of their own strength.

Little hurts more than losing.

What if the losing keeps happening game after game?

That doesn't make youth sports a lost cause for the child experiencing it.

"You want to win; everyone wants to win; everyone wants a ribbon and a trophy and all that," said former NFL player and coach **Herm Edwards**. "But I think it's how you develop when you don't win, because most people are not going to win. You're not going to win every time you play. Now, the intent is to win. And the way you win, I always felt was in the way you prepare, because a lot of things are not under your control.

All you can control is what you do. You can't control the other person, the people you play against. And how you handle that is very important, because sports are an emotional roller coaster. You have to make a lot of decisions in the course of a sporting event then you've got to deal with the consequences of the decision. How do you handle that? To me it creates a mental toughness about yourself, how you handle inconvenience. I always say sports are about inconvenience, like life. People who can handle inconvenience generally have success in life."

That inconvenience was instrumental in Edwards's development.

"It wasn't to the point where if I didn't win I was upset," Edwards said. "It was, 'Why didn't I?' Did I need to improve on something or was the other guy just better than me? In life there's always going to be someone better than you, believe it or not."

In sports as in life, sometimes you can feel you don't really have a chance.

Vonnie Holliday certainly felt that way once. He felt helpless, and then he felt humiliated.

"We were playing a team that was really, really good," Holliday said. "They had some big guys. Looking back, we needed to go back and check their birth certificates because they had to be illegal. There were guys with full beards and mustaches. They were really lining up and kicking our butt, running the ball down our throats."

At halftime, the linebackers coach and defensive coordinator ripped into Holliday and one teammate.

In front of everyone.

"Basically saying that we were soft," Holliday said. "And as a football player, you never want to be called soft."

Especially not in front of teammates and friends.

Especially when, considering the comparative size of the opponent, it wasn't a fair characterization.

"I was embarrassed to the point that I actually teared up and cried at halftime," Holliday said. "I can remember coming out of that half being so pissed off and mad about it that I had to change that view, if that what was what the coach thought about me. I had to let him know that I was not that guy, that I was a *player*. I went out and the second half was totally different. I had a great second half."

The coach pointed out his improvement at the next practice.

"That was a changing point in my play, in my football career, in my football playing days, because I took a huge step that day," Holliday said.

Holliday would step on an NFL field for the first time several years later – and fifteen years after that, he still hadn't stepped off for good.

In sports as in life, a person can be stopped from doing something before even getting started.

That happened to Elton Brand, who as a child was proof that setbacks can not only come in all shapes and sizes but also from not getting in the necessary shape, at least to satisfy a league's participation requirements. He can laugh about it now after all he's accomplished in basketball: a James Naismith Trophy as the nation's best hoops collegian while at Duke University and an NBA Rookie of the Year award. However, at the time it was frustrating to be deemed unfit for another sport. "In Pop Warner football, I weighed too much and couldn't play," Brand said. "I was tall, and I was maybe a little chubby. I wasn't obese or anything, but I couldn't play. They waived the fee for me to play, and I *still* couldn't play because I was too heavy."

In sports as in life, learning a new skill can be a struggle.

Some of the most absurdly blessed and versatile athletes in modern sports history, including **Herschel Walker**, have had trouble doing so. For Walker it was not just once either, and not in just one activity. He "always felt like quitting" as a kid, and he felt those thoughts returning later in life when he tried new pursuits such as bobsledding or tae kwon do or even ballet. "At my first rehearsal, it was so hard, the footwork, and I was thinking of quitting. I thought, 'What in the world am I doing?'" Then, during his early foray into mixed martial arts (MMA), he had the same hesitations. He could have abandoned the endeavor; instead, he won his first MMA fights, two decades after he was a member of the US bobsled team and three decades after he captured the Heisman Trophy.

"You are always going to have doubts," Walker said. "But what you have to do is try to get rid of those doubts."

The trick is getting rid of one's own doubts while channeling the doubts of others, like **Jason Ferguson** did, whose "parents taught me to feed off the negative." He kept feeding on ball carriers, even as a pro, playing thirteen NFL seasons after getting drafted down in the seventh round. But to do that effectively, one must also get rid of the excuses, and adjust one's attitude, in the way that, as we related earlier, Tom Feely ordered grandson Jay to adjust his. As much as a child might wish to always make it all somebody else's fault, that is rarely the reality, and even if it is, it's not a constructive perspective.

In conversations with his seven kids, Allan Houston urges them to be take responsibility and to learn to be adaptable to any situation or environment. He asks about how *they* are behaving and how *they* are treating teammates and cares less about their complaints about playing roles or time. "I think as a parent we get caught judging the system and judging the coaches," Houston said. "And we have to first make sure that we are training our children the right way to approach the sport."

Otherwise children may not stay in the sport for long. Kids who frequently make excuses aren't likely to make the necessary changes to make the situation better. Then, worse, they may decide that the easiest or only choice is to exit from a sport, or sports, entirely.

There are times, as we'll discuss later in the book, when it may be in a child's best interest for an adult to allow that child to discontinue an activity, or for the adult to step in and stop it.

"Maybe the program was lousy and maybe the kid had more foresight to drop out," said **Mark Spitz**, the nine-time Olympic gold medalist swimmer. "Or maybe the kid dropped out because he is not athletically inclined and the program did not develop that set of skills for him, to feel comfortable and confident."

Maybe the sport isn't right.

For instance, not every kid will welcome the contact or culture of tackle football. As former NFL Pro Bowl fullback **Leroy Hoard** argued, the aggressiveness of that game tends to lend itself to a direct, coarse style of teaching it, and all of that – physical and verbal – may be too much for a sensitive young athlete. "You have to fight aggression with aggression," said Hoard, differentiating it from most other sports. "The rules change when you can get hit. Once you get hit, you have to be more aggressive to protect yourself. And you can't be nice to a kid to go out there and get the snot knocked out of him."

Maybe the coach isn't right. Maybe the timing isn't right.

Maybe it's a bit of everything.

That was the case for **Greg Camarillo** in the fifth grade, after his father Al, a history professor at Stanford and former high school football player, warned him on the way to the first day of Pop Warner practice that he might not like it. As it turned out, Greg's father knew best, especially when the coach turned to be a relentless, vulgar screamer. "That was my first exposure to that hardcore mentality, and I hated it, man," said Camarillo, whose father made him stick out only that one season. "That experience discouraged me from wanting to continue to play football. I didn't know if was just the team, or football in general, but I didn't play again for a long time."

It didn't turn out to be football in general. In high school, he felt better prepared to give the sport another shot, encountered coaches who treated players better, and eventually made football into a 10-year professional career.

Maybe quitting is the right move for the child at the moment, since there's usually an opportunity to revisit the decision later.

But as women's basketball great **Cheryl Miller** said, "Make sure you do it for the right reasons. That's because [the child] no longer has that drive or passion."

Not perfect? That's not the right reason. That's not even possible.

Not the best player at the time? That's not necessarily permanent or even the point.

Not pleasing a parent, coach, or teammate in the way one expected to?

"You can't keep everyone happy," Miller said.

No one can.

The athletes we've interviewed were undoubtedly happy they stuck with their sports, from pee wee to preps, and grateful for the influential role that adults played in them. Those adults didn't make them play as much as make them understand why continuing to do so made sense, and how it could help them now and later in all aspects of life. They made it clear that excuses for quitting were unacceptable.

"My parents were very supportive," Karrie Webb said. "I could have said, 'I don't want to play anymore,' as long as it wasn't a reason like, 'This guy I like, he doesn't think golf's cool.'"

The adults made it clear what quitting meant: it meant quitting on oneself.

"My mother always used to say, 'No matter what you do, you always do it at your best,'" Walker said. "She said, 'If you do it, you finish it. I don't care what you start, you finish it.'"

"If I wanted go to, if I wanted to do something, I did it," Maurice Jones-Drew said. "My parents made me finish it all the way through. 'You wanted to do it, so finish it.'"

Not finishing can mean quitting on others.

"With my mom and dad, the only restrictions I had were that I had to get good grades, get my homework done, and not quit," said **Rich Gannon**, the 2002 NFL MVP. "So if I started something at the beginning of the season and I ended up not liking it, my parents felt I had an obligation to the coach and to my teammates to finish it out. I think that is important. I don't think you should let your kids walk away from something, let them learn not to give up on something. The commitment teaches them, the commitment to the other kids that are counting on you as well."

Not finishing can mean quitting on those who care most.

Gabby Reece, a former professional volleyball player, and her husband, pro surfer Laird Hamilton, have exposed their children to sports while being careful not to push. Reece has established just one condition: "If you commit to a team, if I buy all the classes and you tell other people you will be there, then you must complete that [part]. After that, if it's not for you, no problem."

But many kids will find that if they hang on and keep going with the sport, it *is* for them in some form or fashion.

Why didn't **Shannon Sharpe** ever want to quit as a teenager? It was partly because he'd already experienced the alternative. "If I wasn't at football practice, that meant I had to work," the eight-time Pro Bowl tight end said. "You could work or you could have fun. I chose to have fun. And I say this all the time: football was the easiest job I ever had. They fed you your breakfast; they fed you your lunch. You got pizza and donuts on Friday. Man, this is a great job for me."

Sharpe's appetite for the sport only increased as he played. He became one of the millions who found fortitude upon encountering frustration, who built stronger self-esteem through achieving success, and who kept going in a positive direction driven by a dream. Eventually he became the one-in-a-million example of someone who made the most far-fetched athletic dream come true.

SECTION 2:
Why You Matter

"My Biggest Inspiration"

Tony Dorsett had a big dream as a little kid.

It had nothing to do with being a football star. It had everything to do with his household.

"I had four older brothers, and I wanted to be like them," Dorsett said.

Or at least impress them.

In youth football, Tony was a Termite and his next-oldest brother was a Mighty Mite.

"I would come home, and I would make up stories. I would drag my uniform and all that and get it all dirty, and then I said, 'I did this, and I did that,'" Dorsett said. "But I was making it up, because I didn't want to really get out there. I was just doing it because of my brothers."

Then one day Tony's team was playing on a field before his one of his brothers played there. That brother pointed him out to the coach.

"When you're young, the coach is always looking to get everybody in and involved," Dorsett said. "So he looked my way, and I was blown away! I was hiding behind guys. Finally he made me get out there on the kickoff."

Naturally, the kickoff flew straight to him.

"I was scared," Dorsett said. "I got that ball, I took off, and I was like a little rabbit, man. I went like sixty-something, seventy-something yards for a touchdown, untouched, because I was scared to death to get hit. Being such a little kid, I was always afraid. But right there, that got me. That got me. I was like, 'Wow, I can do this.'"

Tony's initial instinct was like that of so many kids. There is a universal human need for acceptance, recognition, and affirmation, the sort that Tony had seen his brothers receive through sports. This led to him emulating them, a process through which he inadvertently uncovered his talent. Eventually he sprinted by them all—all the way to the Pro Football Hall of Fame.

You never know who, or what, in a child's environment will provide a spark—something they value or perceive as valued and then can take in, process, and transform into a desire. Sometimes, in fact, the child isn't even fully aware at the time what is igniting his or her imagination and serving to foster aspiration. For instance, David Eckstein always had a bat in his hand, "and it wasn't like anyone in my family ever played. I knew the starting lineups from the age of three, and I always wanted to play."

Something got that started: identification, imitation, inspiration.

Even if you can't identify the source, you should try to cultivate the child's interest, so long as the activity is positive. You want a child to have the chance to hope and dream, to visualize possibilities grand and small both in the immediate and far-off future. However, you must also help to keep the child grounded enough to remain aware of the work and time required.

You want a child to have the pleasure of a private, protected space to which he or she can retreat and suspend reality, leave negative feelings behind, and picture some desired fantasy. You want to give the child the freedom and comfort to reveal and express those wishes without fear or ridicule, while giving them the opportunity needed to pursue them. You want those dreams to serve as the spark that keeps them working toward something, even if it's not easy at first.

You shouldn't be surprised when a child idealizes, or even fantasizes, about something related to sports.

As a kid, Herm Edwards connected to an old movie about Jim Thorpe, the part-Native American who overcame bigotry to become arguably the greatest athlete of the twentieth century, playing professional football, basketball, and baseball, while winning Olympic gold medals in the pentathlon and decathlon. Thorpe died the year before Edwards was born.

"I wanted to be like that guy," said Edwards, who later became an NFL cornerback and coach. "I wanted to be able to do everything. And that's what I did. If there was a ball involved, I played it. The next guy was Muhammad Ali."

Ali was the Heavyweight Champion of the World, and by many measures, one of the most influential athletes of all time. He was also polarizing due to his political stands and penchant for poetic trash talk. Edwards's father, Herman Sr., was a World War II veteran. "He was disciplined," Herm Jr. said. "He was a Joe Louis fan."

Louis was an Ali predecessor and a more modest, reserved man.

Herman Sr. couldn't understand why his son liked "this big-mouth guy."

"I was like, 'I like this guy because he talked about it and he did it,'" Edwards said. "And I did it too. If you're talking, you better walk it. Those were my guys."

The guys **Brian Jordan** admired were taped all over his bedroom wall, their photos cut out of articles. They were successful athletes of all sorts.

"That's what I wanted to be," said Jordan, now a broadcaster and the author of children's books, including *I Told You I Could Play*. "I would wake up every morning and touch my wall and make the good grades and play sports. And my dreams to play professional sports came true."

Actually, Jordan's dreams came true twice. Jordan would play three seasons as a hard-hitting NFL safety, and then he would play fifteen seasons in Major League Baseball. He made an All-Star game, hit 184 home runs, and drove in more than eight hundred runs. By the time he finished playing, articles about him were taped on a lot of bedroom walls.

Kids wanted to be like Brian Jordan. Of course, even more wanted to be like Michael Jordan. These days, kids want to be LeBron or Peyton or Strasburg or Serena. That dream is a product of society and whom it has conditioned them to admire.

In 1950, Erik Erikson introduced his groundbreaking theory of psychosocial development, one that is still widely studied and followed today. In it he described how external factors in society play an influential role in personality development. Erikson noted that during the preschool years, young children are eager "to emulate ideal prototypes."[8] This explains why they become enamored with fairy tale and comic book heroes, as well as actual people whose talent and celebrity makes them appear larger than life. Given the ubiquity, popularity, and prosperity of sports stars in today's ESPN-driven culture, and the admiration that everyone from peers to parents expresses for those "heroes," it is understandable and perhaps even inevitable that many kids would idolize those athletes, seek to emulate them, and dream to someday become them.

Of course, not every athlete is an appropriate role model or source of inspiration.

This means you need to pose questions.

You should learn more about the athlete's qualities, on and off the playing field, and dig deeper into why the child is drawn in that direction.

---

8   E. H. Erikson, *Childhood and Society* (New York, NY: W. W. Norton & Co., 1950).

Does the child identify with some part of the athlete's story? Why? Does the child appreciate aspects of the athlete's personality or style? Which ones?

Is the athlete unselfish or uncooperative?

Is the athlete unafraid? Unflappable? Unrelenting? Unassuming? Underappreciated?

Undefeated? An underdog?

These insights can be useful, not only to steer the child away from a negative influence but also to better understand how the child views oneself and what he or she finds exciting and motivating.

Sometimes, as embodied by Dorsett's experience, a child finds that inspiration much closer to home—not from some famous person he or she has never met but from someone he or she knows the best. "There were so many people," Edgerrin James said. "The guys who didn't make it, the guys who made it, the family members, your uncles, everybody that could do things that you couldn't actually do. I always looked up to those guys and tried to exceed those people."

Several athletes we interviewed spoke of emulating siblings or cousins who were older but still relatively close in age.

These included former All-Pro linebacker **Cornelius Bennett**, who recalled that he wanted "so, so desperately" to be like his brothers, one of whom excelled at baseball, the other at football. "Whatever they did, I wanted to follow in their footsteps," he said. That was true even when he was getting trampled. His brothers took no pity and made him cry at times. But when they wouldn't let him quit, he realized they were there to help him eventually reach their level. So he kept trying.

Gino Torretta did too, not that he had a choice at first. His three older brothers dragged him to the football field as a kid. "They made me stand in a particular location, not realizing I was practicing, not realizing I was getting better," said Torretta, the 1992 Heisman Trophy winner. "I was getting better by being their punching bag."

Over time, he began to—figuratively—punch back.

Many of the athletes found inspiration in their parents and grandparents and other adult influences who had been athletes themselves. They set out for imitation.

"My dad was my hero," Hall of Fame third baseman **Brooks Robinson** said. "He was a good player, he was a semi-pro player in Little Rock, Arkansas, where I grew up. I went to the same high school, played on the same American Legion team."

Jay Feely's father wrestled in college. Allan Houston's father was a college basketball player and then coach. Chipper Jones's mother was not only an accomplished equestrian but also someone he credits for giving him his "swagger." Grant Hill's father was an NBA star. And so on.

Other athletes took the qualities they admired in another person—those displayed independent of sports—and applied those in an athletic context.

Brandi Chastain's father, Roger, was a supportive presence, trudging off to work as a soda distributor several hours early so he could provide much of the transportation to practices and games for Brandi and her brother Brad. He even coached Brandi's teams for six years after initially knowing little about soccer. To learn, he went to the library and got videotapes.

Yet it was Brandi's mother, Lark, who provided much of her inspiration, and not just because Lark was always present in the bleachers. Brandi was most wowed by what her mother did in boardrooms. "She was a VP of a company in the high-tech arena, in a staffing company working with IBM and Hewlett-Packard, companies that were dominated by men," Brandi said of Lark, who passed in 2002, several months before Roger did. "Right there I had a living role model, that showed me if you wanted something, you should move forward to it. She would also embarrass the heck out of me wherever we were because she didn't take no for an answer. For her there was always a solution to a problem. I think that was one of the greatest gifts she's given me. Other people would see roadblocks; I just see answers."

Many of the athletes saw, in a caregiver, persistence and perseverance in the face of challenges that had nothing to do with sports. And then they mimicked those models in a different setting: sports. They developed an athletic drive, in a passion to accomplish something that would impress or even surpass those they respected, with that passion carrying through childhood and well into adulthood.

While at the 2012 NBA Legends Brunch at All-Star Weekend in Orlando, **Penny Hardaway** said, "That's the story for myself and a lot of guys in this room."

Hardaway noted that many had been motivated by the work ethic instilled by hard-working parents. "For me, I just had my grandmother," Hardaway said. "I looked up to her because I saw how hard she worked, and that kind of pushed me."

O.J. McDuffie had his mother Gloria.

"What she did as a single parent means there is nothing I can't achieve," said McDuffie, who played ten seasons at receiver for the Miami Dolphins. "Having me as a teenager, going to school and to college, getting her Masters … how could I not succeed after seeing all she did?"

Dwight Stephenson had both parents.

"My mother and father, I watched them work and struggle all of their life to provide and make things possible for the family," said Stephenson, the Pro Football Hall of Fame center. "They were my biggest inspiration."

He put pressure on himself to make it, for himself and for them.

Bruce Smith did the same for his family. Like many of the athletes we interviewed, he was motivated by challenging environmental circumstances and the possibility that sports participation could serve as a vehicle to mitigate and, perhaps eventually, escape them. His story is a testament to the power that sports possess, in connecting a child's inspiration – through perspiration – to the fulfillment of some aspiration.

"In my particular case, I had two parents that came from very modest beginnings and very modest means," Smith said. "They made minimum wage, both of them often having second jobs, doing odds and ends jobs to make ends meet. I saw the struggles and sacrifices they made on a daily basis for my brother and my other two siblings. It gave me a greater appreciation for what they did in their lives and their struggles, and they were not necessarily enjoying the work or the mentality that they had. But they knew they had to do it to provide for their family."

Smith grew up in a tough area and attended an inner-city school where teasing and bullying were the norm. In addition to living up to the model set by his parents, he wished to be accepted and respected by his peers. Football became a source of self-worth, and also a driver of it. "I found my confidence and a strong self-esteem by preparing, working out, striving to reach a goal, and taking those steps to accomplish that goal," Smith said. "It is powerful."

Nothing is more powerful as a source of inspiration than the dream of a better life, whether that dream comes from a child, is held by someone else *for* the child, or is held *by* the child for someone else. In **Curtis Martin**'s case, all three came together, though he, unlike others in this book, didn't initially see sports as the way to improve his situation. What a horrifying situation it was. In his candid 2012 Pro Football Hall of Fame induction speech, with his mother, Rochelle, in attendance, Martin spoke of his traumatic childhood: his father's verbal and physical abuse of his mother, the murder of his grandmother, the illness and death of his aunt, the fear and loneliness of time alone in an empty apartment, and even a near-death experience when a gun was pointed at his head.

"A lot of my friends were getting in trouble," Martin said. "My best friend had gotten killed."

So few had hope for his future by the time he got to high school.

Rochelle, however, did not waver.

She kept holding onto that dream for him, no matter who or what tried to knock it away.

"My mother said, 'I don't care what you do, but you are going to do *something* after school so you are not around the neighborhood all the time,'" Martin said. "So she told me I had no choice if there was a spelling bee club, or basketball, football, baseball, something. My mother was a forceful person. She speaks her mind. You are going to listen to her. So she kinda pushed me out the door."

Mark Wittgartner, the gym teacher and football coach, opened his, simply by showing interest. And so, football became that "something," not because Curtis thought he would enjoy it, wanted to appease two adults who cared about him in a world with too few such people.

Curtis got plenty of yards, breaking records as a senior to earn a scholarship to the University of Pittsburgh, a scholarship he initially didn't want to accept since he wasn't all that fond of sports or studying. Then, after not wanting to join the NFL, Curtis became one of its all-time leading rushers. On that level he found the discipline-oriented male role model he craved in then-Patriots coach Bill Parcells, and even if he never got all that much fulfillment from the game, he got a chance—through his earnings and profile—to get something that mattered even more. He got to give a better life not only to himself and his mother but also to many others who came from circumstances he recognized. With his Curtis Martin Job Foundation, Martin has provided financial aid and hands-on support to single mothers, children's charities, individuals with disabilities, and low-income housing providers.

As Martin said near the end of his Hall of Fame speech, "When I realized that football was a vehicle, I used it to impact people's lives and do positive things."

Martin represents an extreme exception compared to many of those we interviewed in two ways: his traumatic childhood, and his initial and continued lack of passion and related ambition when it came to sports. Still, he is similar to all of our other interviewees in one sense: his rise to exceptional heights, rarefied air that no parent or adult should reasonably expect a child to reach, no matter how inspired, motivated, ambitious, talented, or enamored by sports that child may be. The chances that a child will someday play in a professional arena or stadium are infinitesimal, even if everything breaks right and the child gets the best of all the unpredictable, uncontrollable, and unrelated variables, from genetics to luck to coaching to health.

Still, none of that means that anyone should extinguish a child's enthusiasm or stamp out their dream. It is better to let the playing play out and see where the inspiration leads the child. Even if it doesn't lead to a lifelong and lucrative career, or even to an athletic scholarship, it might add a joyful, educational element to a child's life.

Take Karrie Webb. When she was eleven, she received a combined Christmas and birthday present from her grandparents: tickets to a men's golf tournament featuring a fellow Australian, Greg Norman, who was ranked number one in the world. Upon returning from the tournament, she told her parents that she had her sights set on someday turning professional in golf. "It seemed like a pipe dream to a lot of people in my small town," Webb said. "They would respond, 'That's great, but if it doesn't work out, what do you want to do?' But I never really looked back from that."

Nor did Karrie's parents ever look at her wish as silly.

Consider the case of **Carlos Boozer**. He wasn't a prime candidate to become an NBA player. He hailed from Alaska, hardly a hoops hotbed. Still, he wanted to play. He wanted to see where his talent took him. His parents did not take his spirit away.

"They did not discourage me," Boozer said. "They didn't tell me, 'Why do you want to play basketball? That's a pipe dream; one in a billion kids make it.' They said, 'Okay, do you mind going to a camp?' I said I wanted to go to every camp. So I am seven, eight, nine, ten, eleven, going to camps all over the place—Alaska camps, California camps, camps in New Jersey, all over the place. But I was blessed to have parents who let me follow my dream. I would advise parents to let your kid follow a dream, even if it's not sports."

Let them but also lead them.

Lead them the way that Johnny Alexander led Bennie Blades.

For decades, Alexander coached the Western Tigers in the smallest varsity division in the West Lauderdale Football Club of the Hollywood Optimist League. He served as a father figure for many kids who were without one, molding them into future high school, collegiate, and professional stars. And he served as an extra set of eyes outside the home, even for those who lived with two parents.

"He got me, fortunately, at seven years old," Blades said.

Alexander also got Blades's brother Brian when the latter was eight.

"It was not about him or the game," Bennie Blades said. "It was about you the individual. If you want something out of life, what you put into it is what you're going to get out of it."

Alexander needed to work to get more out of Bennie.

"I had very low self-esteem," Blades said. "I was awkward; my brothers were the athletic ones. My brothers always said I was the nerdy kid."

So Bennie didn't think he had the ability to accomplish much in sports. Alexander had higher hopes—and shared them with Bennie. That proved inspirational and motivational.

"He said, 'It doesn't matter what everyone else does,'" Blades recalled. "'This is what you develop within yourself. That's what matters. It's not about who is most athletic. It's about the kid who tries the hardest. That is the kid who is the most resilient; that is the kid who is going to make it. It's not about what's outward. It's about what's inward, and you want to bring that outward.'"

Alexander's lesson was grounded in the sports psychology principle of intrinsic motivation: the coach encouraged Bennie to take pride in trying his best, even if it didn't necessarily mean being the best, at least not at that stage. As Bennie improved, his pride swelled, and that improvement was noticed and lauded by others. That momentum built upon itself so much that it took Blades toward elite collegiate and professional careers.

But he never forgot where it started. It started with someone from outside catalyzing something he was feeling inside. This is an illustration of the trust progression that you can attempt to replicate: the belief *of* an adult and the belief *in* an adult, serving as the two seeds that can sprout into the child's belief in him or herself.

"Someone Was Behind Me"

UDONIS HASLEM came up short. Or so he thought.

"I was playing with some older guys," Haslem recalled. "And I took a shot. And it was an air ball."

The ball could have crashed to the concrete, taking Udonis's confidence down with it. "That would have embarrassed me," the Miami Heat forward conceded. But on that day, as on so many others, the eleven-year-old was not alone. He was playing on the same side as someone he trusted, someone who was more than sixteen years older, but who had consistently set an example that someone still growing could clearly understand and appreciate. He was playing with his stepbrother Sam Wooten.

"He was a selfless person," Haslem said. "He did for other people. He sacrificed his own goals and dreams. Instead of going to college to play ball, he worked to help my stepmom. He also worked part time as a tutor to help people. And he treated me like a real baby brother. He took me to the basketball court and really invested a lot of time in me. My parents had to work very hard, and he was the one taking me under his wing, taking me to the court every day."

That often meant Wooten taking his little stepbrother on his team, like he had that day when the ball hung up in the air. That day when he caught it, and then dunked it. That made Udonis look good. But that was also the easy part, just an instinctive athletic move.

What mattered more? Making sure Udonis *felt* good.

"Good pass," Sam told him.

That statement may not seem like much, but to Udonis it was everything.

It remains one of the fondest memories that Haslem has of Wooten, who died in 1999 and never had a chance to see his kid stepbrother become a three-time NBA champion and the Heat's all-time rebounding leader. Haslem wears the initials "SW" on his shoes but acknowledges Wooten's imprint goes far beyond that. For all the family upheaval and tragedy that Haslem encountered in his early years, he developed a strong belief in himself, a belief that has allowed him to disprove doubters and overcome obstacles as a collegian and a professional.

"I wasn't given much in life," Haslem said.

Yet he was given something priceless.

He was given a winning tie—a connection that provided enduring comfort.

Win, lose, or draw, that's what most kids really need.

Udonis was given the knowledge and security that someone cared for him and believed in him. He was given a strong teammate off the court as well as on. Someone who provided unconditional support. Someone who accepted and empathized with feelings, regardless of the circumstances. Someone who comforted and encouraged. Someone who made him feel safe and protected, win or lose. Someone he could count on to back and prop him up. Someone who recognized and empowered his dreams, whatever those were and from wherever they came. Someone he could trust. Someone who gave him more reasons to trust in himself.

What is trust? It is the confidence in the availability, concern, and intentions of another. It is an evolving process that should start in infancy, before the baby even knows what a parent is, but becomes familiar with a certain touch, voice, presence or routine. It can occur with others as a child grows, the onset depending on the setting, duration, and frequency of interaction. Trust can strengthen as the child not only receives consistent care, appropriate discipline and unconditional love but begins to better process the nature of the relationship with the other person. Conversely, trust can deteriorate if a child experiences anything that undermines a sense of safety and security with someone.

How does trust relate to youth sports?

It is at the heart of everything.

Ideally, trust is established well before a child starts youth sports. If a child feels comfortable with a particular caregiver, that comfort can grow through shared experiences in other play spaces. If the child is confident that that you, as that nurturing other, care about his or her well-being, that child will likely believe that you are offering new "play" opportunities for *some* good reason, even if the reason isn't completely clear. That child will embrace the new experience almost solely on your endorsement.

Ideally that trust in you will grow as the child embarks on and progresses through the youth sports levels and challenges—provided that you are serving as support all along the sometimes rocky and uneven path. And, ideally, the child will learn to trust other nurturing figures present in the youth sports environment, those also trying to make a difference while the ball is in the air.

So many of the athletes we interviewed were fortunate enough to have one or more sufficiently healthy attachment while growing up, and their recollections highlighted the critical importance of those connections in their youth sports progression. Some of the athletes were raised in what is commonly considered a conventional family structure. Ed "Too Tall" Jones, Steve Largent, Cheryl Miller, Dan Marino, and Mario Lemieux are among those who had two biological parents under the same roof throughout their adolescence. Many, however, didn't have the opportunity to establish a close relationship with both. Some didn't even have the opportunity to establish a relationship with one.

Still, in so many of the situations we observed, somebody stepped up to steer a child in the right direction. For Andre Dawson, a grandmother served as the guiding force. For many, it was a brother, sister, uncle, aunt, or stepparent. For others, a coach, teacher, or community figure did the job.

Andre Ware, just seven when his father died of pneumonia, found a father figure in a high school coach, Doug Ferris, who "told it like it was" and allowed players to "wrap your hands" around the truth. **Alonzo Mourning** credited his foster mother, Fannie Threet, the woman who raised him after he chose not to live with either of his divorced parents and who over the years raised fifty others like him.

"I had the right people in my life at the right time," Mourning said. "The right influences."

As a kid, **David Bowens** didn't seem likely to find stability or hope anywhere. He bounced from foster home to foster home in Michigan after his mother put him up for adoption, and after a family took him in at age six, his adoptive father died of a heart attack. His adoptive mother remarried a few years later, and David came to idolize his adoptive stepfather, in part for Frank Williams' bowling prowess. Just as critical to David's development was "being forced to go to the Boys and Girls Club." There he found admirable adults, opportunities to be active, an alternative to "wandering off" and "screwing up," and new friends who would compete with him athletically at the most unstable point of his journey toward a twelve-year NFL career.

Caron Butler, who was dealing drugs at age eleven and had been arrested fifteen times by age fifteen, found structure and support through counselors at the Brace Center in Racine, Wisconsin. "What I liked about the organization and everything was that they were so hands on. They took the craft so seriously; it was just about making us people. It was not about making us great professional athletes in whatever field we chose but making sure we understood life values and life skills. It just made us better in general. That was the biggest lesson I learned: just how to be a great person."

LeBron James is one of the world's greatest athletes, but the world might never have known him if he hadn't encountered some truly great adults. They were those concerned most about making him a champion in life, regardless of what he accomplished on a court or field.

"Mentors are the biggest thing, someone who really cares for the kid," said James, the 2012 *Sports Illustrated* Sportsman of the Year.

As a kid LeBron hardly had an idyllic existence. His father, an ex-con, left when he was a baby. His doting grandmother passed. His young single mother struggled. His address changed and changed and changed again. His school attendance greatly suffered.

"Looking back on my situation, I was very blessed I was able to have guys like Dru Joyce and Frank Walker Sr., to be my youth coaches," James said. "Not only did they teach us about sports, they taught us about being young men and having responsibilities and things like that."

James credits Frank Walker Sr., an Akron Housing Authority employee as well as a coach, for being the first man to put a football, and then a basketball, in his hands in an organized athletic setting. But Frank Walker Sr., and his wife, Pam, did much more than that for him—and much of it in their home. At first, their son Frankie didn't like LeBron, annoyed that this "huge, hulking kid" dashed his dream of starting at running back on their Akron peewee team. Eventually, though, they became brothers, as Frank Sr. and Pam made LeBron feel like family.

"I spent Christmas with them every single year up until I was in high school," James said. "They fed me every day. They gave me chores too."

In fifth grade, LeBron spent weeknights with them. During the day, he was at school. The Walkers made sure of that. He recorded perfect attendance.

"They gave me responsibility, structure, and stability when me and my mother … she was always trying to find a living," James said.

They gave him lessons he would take into the rest of his life.

In all of the above cases, kids heeded lessons because they trusted the adults imparting them.

Blood relative? Sports aficionado? Same gender?

It doesn't much matter.

What matters is that the kids had someone who was with them along the way, someone serving as a safety net as they went through the evolving childhood cycle of growth and development.

Like **Rafer Alston** did.

His father, Richard, had drug problems and wasn't around to see a nine-year-old Rafer score thirty-eight of his team's thirty-nine points in a Catholic Youth Organization game. Mike Bell, the coach, did. Bell saw more than that. The counselor for wayward boys saw the boy's potential as a person and accepted Rafer's request to serve as a surrogate father. Bell even took Rafer in for a while and kept him occupied and engaged by showing him basketball videos.

"He always believed I had a gift to really make it in this game at an early age," said Alston, who became a playground legend before playing for a decade in the NBA and even starting in the 2009 NBA Finals. "I had to overcome a lot of off the court things, as far as moving from home to home and growing up in a tough environment like New York City. As I went to high school, he saw something really special in me. Even when I struggled at school, he kept on pushing. He said, 'Keep working hard, never give up, don't stop.' Then I had friends who were always with me every step of the way. They kept being so positive with me. 'You are going to make it. Keep working.'"

At times, as a child and as an adult, Rafer has tested the patience of those who care about him, doing some damage to his name along the way. But it's unlikely anyone outside of New York City would have ever known his name if not for the support he received early on.

"I know it's a fine line, because you also want to discipline the kid," Alston said. "If you continue to shoot him down, shoot him down, that is when the kid is going to believe he's nothing."

It's far better that someone makes the kid believes he's something.

A coach did this for another New York-produced point guard, **Mark Jackson.**

When he was seven, Mark wasn't any good at basketball.

"My first year I scored one point the entire year," Jackson said.

That might not seem like much. However, to Jackson it was as meaningful as anything he would accomplish later on as a star guard at St. John's University, an NBA Rookie of the Year for the New York Knicks, a starter for the Indiana Pacers in the NBA Finals, and now the coach of the Golden State Warriors. The way that accomplishment made him feel—that he had done something extraordinary, that he belonged—may have made all the rest possible. "If I went back to that one foul shot that I hit … my coach jumped and grabbed me, high-fived me, my teammates were going crazy," Jackson said. "And I was jumping up and down like I had just won Game 7 of the [NBA] Finals. But the thing is that *everybody* was in it. I can remember that moment as if it was yesterday, and it was almost forty years ago. But it propelled me."

In retrospect, Jackson is glad that he wasn't given playing time that he hadn't earned.

"No, I played at the *end* of the game," Jackson said. "Otherwise I would have been robbing the good guys. Instead of giving me something that I didn't deserve, that made me work for it. And it got me to say, 'I'm not satisfied with that one point. Next year, I'm coming back and I'm going to do better.'"

This is the way you want the cycle to unfold. It starts with some sort of inspiration which, once assimilated, becomes the wish or dream. That dream creates the initiative to get started and do what's necessary to become competent. That competence, once recognized by oneself and by others, can solidify self-esteem and, along with enjoyment, provide the impetus to keep practicing and competing. That repetition, in practices and games, may lead to even greater mastery which, over time, can stimulate even bigger dreams, thus starting the cycle again on the way to fostering even greater accomplishment.

You, as a caring adult, need not merely act as a bystander to this cycle.

You can help set it in motion, and help it along.

You can do so, in a youth sports context, simply by showing up.

There are few better ways to earn a child's trust than to show interest in an activity, and there are few better feelings for a child than to spot a trusted ally in the bleachers. Watching. Hoping. Smiling. Clapping.

Universally, kids have a yearning for this sort of acknowledgement and attention. When James McKnight took his young kids to the pool, they would call his name one hundred times. And if he didn't take notice of all their little flips, they'd yell, "Daddy, Daddy, Daddy, you didn't watch me. You didn't see. I want to do it again."

It doesn't really matter if you're a fan of the sport or understand little of what you're watching. You merely must understand what your presence means to a child.

"My parents were always there for me every practice, game, and tournament," said **Mario Lemieux**, a Hockey Hall of Famer. "That's where it starts."

"They were in the stands. They were there, always supporting me," Gino Torretta said. "I think that is the thing for the parent. It's not just the coach. You have to be there supporting your kids. 'Here I am.' To me that is the most important thing."

"My dad was my best coach ever," Dan Marino said. "He was there almost every day."

As Cornelius Bennett put it, "When kids see an adult watching them, they tend to do their best."

That can be the case even if the adult isn't related. In the small Georgia town where Sam Madison grew up, there were always plenty of proxies. "Everybody pretty much knew everybody, so all our parents took care of us kids," Madison said. "No matter who I was playing against, they always encouraged us. That was one thing, having the community relationship. It pushed all of us, having that care we needed. When my parents weren't there, I had someone else's parents pushing and driving me. They always wanted us to succeed. They were always there watching us."

When adults are watching, kids tend to feel their best. They feel valued. They feel like what they are doing matters to someone else in their life as much as it matters to them.

Vonnie Holliday's single mother had to work, but the family made sure that someone—often an older sister—got him to practice. All women of the Holliday household did what they could to get to his games.

As a child **Channing Crowder** had limited contact with his father, Randy, who played in the NFL but then spent time in jail on a drug conviction and ultimately divorced Channing's mother, Pauline. Channing was frustrated when he first started playing football, because he preferred to touch the ball as a running back, and the coaches stuck him at the thankless position of defensive nose guard.

"I didn't know what the hell I was doing," Crowder said.

His mother, Pauline, told him to keep trying. She never acted like taking him to practice, where he could learn to improve, was a hassle. She bought him cleats, wristbands, and gloves even when cash was tight.

"Not much words but just the support," Crowder said. "Just knowing that someone was behind me and believed in me kept me going."

As he kept going, so did his mother and sisters—to stadiums of all sizes.

"Knowing they are there to support you, you try to impress your family, really," Crowder said. "My mom didn't miss a game until I got to the NFL. She went to every Pop Warner game, every high school game, away, home, every college game, away, home."

In today's busy world, it's understood that not every parent can be Pauline Crowder.

Even if you can't be everywhere at once, you can still "show up" in other ways.

You can show up with your selflessness.

When **Luis Gonzalez**, who grew up in a house of women in Tampa, Florida, recalled how his mother and grandmother "were always there" in the context of his sports development, he wasn't necessarily referring to their physical presence. "We didn't have a lot of money, and it always seemed like if there was some type of sporting equipment I needed. They were always sacrificing something so I could go on the field," said the five-time Major League Baseball All-Star. "And I always appreciated that."

You, as the caring adult, can show up with your curiosity. That means making it clear to the child that you care about his or her sports schedules, teammates, coaches, triumphs, struggles, conflicts, likes, and dislikes. If your schedule simply won't allow you to always observe or even inquire in person, you can leverage modern technology. While a text, call or even FaceTime session may not be quite the same as being there, it's all far better than nothing—especially when your focus in those forums is on whether the child had a good time and was pleased with a performance, rather than on who won or lost. This shows the child that you always keep him or her in mind, even when you may be out of sight.

You can show up even when, in terms of sports knowledge or acumen, you are initially out of your league.

"My dad, he would drive me and show up to the competitions," Shannon Miller said. "My father wouldn't know a cartwheel from a contango. But I knew he was interested. My mom, she showed her interest in a different way. But that's the important thing: showing interest."

Miller's mother set out to learn gymnastics' lingo so she could more fully understand all facets of her daughter's skills, tasks, movements, and language. Miller's family didn't have much money, so her father would shoot video, allowing her mother to review the competitions later.

"She got so into it that she started doing some coaching and judging," Miller said. "She ended up finding a love through those two things, through my love of the sport."

But Miller's mother didn't overdo it either.

"I think it's critical that they be part of the process," Miller said. "It was good that my mother worked a full-time job, so she couldn't sit around with me at every practice. It allowed me to venture out and find friends and not just go to Mommy."

Ted Walton never developed the love for basketball that Claudia Miller did for gymnastics. He simply loved his son enough to endorse the pursuit. "I never shot a basket with my dad," said **Bill Walton**, a Basketball Hall of Famer and NBA broadcaster. "My dad is the most unathletic person I ever saw in my life. I saw him run one time at the church picnic and I fell over laughing. I graduated from UCLA thirty-seven years ago. My parents to this day ask me, 'Say, Billy, did you ever get a job?' I am closer than ever before to saying yes."

The Waltons' divergent interests didn't stop them from being close.

"It is the children's lives," Walton said. "The job of the parent is the same job as the coach. Let them play. It is their game. Be positive, encouraging, supporting, loving, and let them play."

You can show up by knowing when to step back, trusting the child to discover and develop a passion while also assessing and assisting the child's progress. You can do this best if you do some digging, acquiring as much knowledge as possible about the child and the experience. You can do that best through frequent, attentive, and effective communication, something that can be a challenge even for those with the purest intentions to always do well.

"Listen"

CLIFF FLOYD had everything, in abundance.

Everything you might think would fortify him against any insecurity. Size, strength, ability.

All of that made him a three-sport star at Thornwood High in South Holland, prior to a lengthy career in the Major Leagues, which began when the Montreal Expos selected him in the first round in 1991 and finally ended in 2009.

If you associate those admired athletic qualities with emotional security, and if you assume that security would translate into smugness or conceit, you might find this difficult to accept: from childhood into adulthood, Floyd preferred to shrink into the shadows.

"Even though everyone thought that I was this or that, or that I was outspoken, I was the shyest," Floyd said. "Unbelievably shy. I tried to stay away from everything. I just wanted people to know that I wasn't cocky or arrogant. I hated attention. I hated anything that was attention on me. I think there were times when I actually didn't want to do so well, because I didn't want any spotlight. I really didn't. I don't care what sport it was, basketball, baseball. I wanted to miss a dunk or strike out three times, because I hated that at the end of the day the spotlight would be on me. I did not want to say two words, or hear my teammates tell me how well I did that day, or whatever the case may be."

Nothing in Floyd's environment would necessarily suggest he would end up feeling and acting this way. Unlike many of the aforementioned athletes in this book, and so many kids from the south side of Chicago, he was blessed to come from a stable home in a decent neighborhood. Floyd enjoyed a loving relationship with both parents. His father, Cornelius, a U.S. Steel employee and former Marine, was his biggest booster. Cornelius, formerly a fine ballplayer himself, would attend Cliff's games even while dealing with kidney failure that would require a transplant.

His mother, Olivia, while working to further support the family, was the driving force behind Cliff's determination, teaching him even as a young athlete not to fear failure or quit trying.

In previous sections, we stressed the importance of showing up as well as showing interest, and certainly the Floyds fully qualified as exemplary parents in those areas. Yet there's more to it. Shortly after his playing career concluded and while he transitioned into broadcasting, Floyd reconsidered his childhood, and specifically the manner in which his parents had communicated with him. His assessments illustrate how the more consistently and clearly an adult communicates with a child, the more likely a message will be heard and accepted—or, at the least, the better the adult will understand how the child processes what he or she takes in. Further, the better the adult and child come to understand each other through these interactions, the better the adult will understand how to communicate in the future.

"I think for me the most important thing is for a parent, grandparent, or anyone involved to listen to what that kid has to say," Floyd said. "To me that was important. Because, now being a parent, I look back on it. You [as a kid] have a lot going on, and you just want someone to hear you out. Just listen for five minutes as opposed to the one who goes 'rrrrr' and talks to you. My dad got it real good. My mom didn't get it so well, in my opinion. That was the only thing I thought that I wished for more, and I wish, in looking back on it now, I am doing it right today. You hear so many people say, 'Wow, he's such a good listener,' and that touches home for me. I feel like when you hear somebody and you can listen to what they said and apply it to what they say and mean, that is so important."

Why was it so important to Cliff?

"It was more to understand who I was as a kid," Floyd said. "In my mind, I was a totally different kid. I can't really explain it—how different I was. I wasn't different in terms of being better, but I looked at these kids and knew I was different. I didn't want any friends, you know what I mean?"

Nor did he seek the adulation that came with success. In that sense, his preference was at odds with his mother's pressure. He didn't really want to be good, yet felt she wouldn't be satisfied with great. While his father, who passed away in 2007, was "the most lenient, chill dude" who knew as a former athlete what they faced, "my mom was just a mom who expected a ton out of her son."

Did she push him to play?

"Mom pushed me in a different way," Floyd said. "She thought that I should hit 1.000. Really! Not like .900. She thought that I should be better than Michael Jordan. She thought I should be the best player that ever touched the field in baseball."

Even if that was not what he desired.

"We never saw eye to eye on it," Floyd said.

And yet, over the years, and even long into adulthood, Floyd came to begrudgingly accept it. He had been raised to respect his parents, and he respected that relationship enough to keep many of his thoughts inside. He decided that one day he would subtly joke about his discomfort with his mom's disconnect and see if she caught on.

"Haha, maybe she will get it," Floyd said. "She didn't. I left it alone."

He returned to it in his late thirties when his athletic career was over.

"We had a talk about the old days," Floyd said. "I remember this, I remember this, and I remember when you never used to hear me out. She actually listened. I thought, 'Wow!' She said, 'I wish now that I had, because that made so much sense to me now.' I thought, 'Damn, I wish I could have said this when I was sixteen.'"

That unrealized wish didn't stop Floyd from achieving professional success, even while dealing with an assortment of injuries, or from continuing to love and admire his mother as a grown man. Still, as we've emphasized throughout the book, such ends—especially athletic ones—shouldn't be the measure of whether a particular approach was right with a particular child. A different style of communication, one that better acknowledged and accounted for Cliff's unique personality, might have made him feel more at ease throughout his youth and into adulthood.

However, it is easier to make that assessment from afar than from inside a relationship. Even for those with the best intentions, communication can be a conundrum, requiring constant review and revision. Communication between any two parties is complex, especially in a modern era in which adults are dealing with so many other daily distractions that make it a challenge to focus sole attention on any single situation or individual. Communication, then, is not just a two-way street, as it's often incorrectly characterized. It's more like a congested highway interchange with numerous overpasses and exits, marked by obstacles, potholes, detours, and ditches. Conversations and interactions can be fraught with misunderstandings and misinterpretations.

This is especially true when it comes to communication between an adult and a child, since kids can't possibly know or process everything that might be affecting an adult and aren't often willing to verbally share everything they are feeling with that adult. A child's actions can speak louder and clearer than words. For example, one of the most powerful ways a child communicates, particularly in response to an adult's mixed message that has produced feelings of anger, is to use the silent treatment. Children often use this tactic with the hope that such an unspoken message might ring louder in the parent's ears. What would induce this? Imagine, for instance, telling a child that you aren't upset with the way he or she played, but doing so with a frown or praising another child's performance in comparison. What is the child supposed to think? How is the child supposed to react? It is critical for an adult to understand that communication isn't simply what you are saying, publicly from the sidelines or privately during the car ride home, or what the child is saying to you. It is the tone with which each of you are saying it, and the mannerisms and gestures intentionally or even inadvertently used to accompany what is expressed verbally.

The average child is not capable of uncluttering the communication airwaves. That's on you, the adult, to clear out the static. It's up to you to adjust the manner in which you address the child, to best limit the chance that he or she misreads or mishears what you are presenting.

It's up to you to put in the effort, not only in addressing the younger person but also in listening with your ears, eyes, mind, and heart—and your memory of being a child. And it's up to you to abandon your assumptions and to understand that no circumstance, however similar, is exactly the same as what you experienced. Just because you reacted a certain way at a certain time, it does not mean all children will react the same way.

"The biggest thing is finding a way to communicate with the younger generation," said NBA player **Roger Mason Jr.** "Lots of times, as you get older, you see that you don't always do things the way you were taught. You want kids to see it from your perspective. I think sometimes we have to be more creative as mentors and try to get to their level. Maybe we should approach the points and issues that we face through their eyes, dumbing it down a bit to make it simpler. Sometimes when I was younger, I did not quite understand what [adults] were trying to tell me, but they were explaining it to me the way they were taught."

Maybe another kid on Mason's team would have understood. But that is the thing: all kids are different.

It's up to you, most of all, to understand *that*.

This is true if you are the caregiver or, in this day and age of American diversity, if you are the coach. When **James Jones**, a 10-year NBA veteran, grew up in urban Miami, many of his teammates came from similarly disadvantaged situations, whether that meant a parent was missing or money was scarce. In some ways, that made it easier for a coach to relate to all players in somewhat similar fashion. "I think, a lot of kids today, outside of the inner city, the backgrounds and the family situations are mixed, you have more interracial couples, you have more Hispanic kids," Jones said. "So it's a melting pot now on the youth scene and different cultures and different parenting techniques force coaches to alter and be more flexible in their methods."

While that is useful to acknowledge, the reality is that no two kids, even those with similar genes or from the same household, are exactly identical in terms of their interests, abilities, dispositions, sensitivities, and motivations. "Just like [the coach] Jimmy Johnson always said, 'Treat everyone differently but fairly,'" Jason Taylor said. "It's the same thing with kids. You can't treat everyone the same."

That's because, as Phillies shortstop **Jimmy Rollins** noted, "Everybody's different."

Different kids will react to adult supervision or interjection differently.

"Some kids just don't want their parents involved," Rollins said.

Certain kids may feel that way because their parents aren't listening to what they're saying or acting appropriately. Certain kids are just easily embarrassed by anything that their parents do. Certain kids would simply rather not be pushed anywhere, while others might tolerate it in one setting, like a classroom, but not in another, like the playing field.

"Some kids want to be pushed," Rollins said.

Tim Hudson wanted to be challenged as a kid, especially when on the field. It wasn't because he expected to someday play professional baseball, to say nothing of making three All-Star teams. After all, at age eight, that ambition seemed no more likely to him than "a space shuttle trip to Mars." And it wasn't because his parents were prone to applying special pressure. "I'm sure as a kid I probably joked with my parents, or my parents joked with me, 'Hey, you're my little big leaguer,' but it was never serious." It was just because Hudson loved playing. He wanted to play better, and for him and his particular developing personality, a little hard work and tough love were well worth it.

"I always felt like I could do better," he said. "I always felt like I should have done better. I think that's one reason why a lot of players are good: they are never satisfied with where they are."

In the same vein, O.J. McDuffie responded well to his uncle's approach to teaching sports. "He reinforced a lot of my skills and he's the one that worked with me on everything," McDuffie said of Homer. "But more than anything, he was critical of everything I did. Even as a little kid, he concentrated on the negative more than he would on the positive just so I could get better at everything I did. My uncle always said 'You can always get better.' I think that's what really carried me along, was he was always stressing, 'You are never good *enough*. You can always get better.'"

Still, adults need to be careful not to get carried away, and assume that sort of mentoring style will work with every child the way it worked with young O.J. Not every child responds as he did. And not every child responds at a certain age, the way he or she would at an earlier or later age.

"I think my dad did a real good job when I was young; it wasn't as serious," NBA veteran **Raja Bell** said. "I had fun, and it was all positive reinforcement. As soon as I got older and I was able to take constructive criticism, he'd bring things to my attention. I did not always take it very well, but at that point, you can handle it because it's preparing you to go further. So there is a time and a place for that. It is kind of a tightrope parents have to walk; otherwise it can be too much and turn a kid off."

Gino Torretta felt like he was always walking a tightrope with his mother, Connie, in terms of what she would deem an acceptable performance on a given day.

"She made sure to point out my weaknesses, from my batting swing in little league to [much later]," Torretta said. "I can remember through my junior year at the University of Miami; we played [the University of] Houston on a Thursday night. I had four touchdowns in the first half. The first thing she said after I came out of the tunnel: 'You weren't even 50 percent in the second half.' By then, I was twenty years old."

How would other kids have handled Connie's approach? Especially other *young* kids?

"That is probably a fine line," Torretta said. "The parents have got to realize, 'Okay, how far can I push to where my child doesn't turn away from me?' That is probably the hardest thing for a parent. You want them to get better, you want them to do it, but you don't know when it is going to click or when everything is going to come together."

You can't know that, or much of anything, in absolute terms. Not all kids are transparent with feelings, or are even immediately aware of all the ways something may be affecting them. "When you play youth football, the worst it probably got was coaches screaming, 'You don't want to be soft, you're not going to let them punk us, you need to be a man, you're playing like little girls,'" James Jones said. "Either way you slice it, some kids just don't respond to positive reinforcement, but I don't think *any* kid responds to negative berating. Some kids may respond physically, but *mentally* it catches up to them."

There are simply too many variables for there to be a fool-proof, catch-all communication approach that an adult can apply effectively to every situation with every child.

Generally, however, a good place to start is to recognize that showing is better than yelling, and thus, to follow Edgerrin James' advice: "Pulling kids aside, this is what you have to do." That's what worked for David Bowens after he got too high on himself ("I thought I was gold") and was demoted from captain as a senior in high school. "You have to get on the level of the kid as an adult so they understand where you're coming from," Bowens said. "What my coach did was he sat me down. He told me, 'This is what we expect of you. Even though you're good and people say this about you, there's a certain expectation.' You don't necessarily have to have an [arm's-length] child-teacher relationship all the time. Sometimes that kid needs to know where you are coming from, so when he is criticized or patted on the back, he doesn't take it the wrong way. Communication is the critical thing."

And yet communication is not something you can do just one way, in every situation, with everyone. So much of communication is trial and error and adjustment on the fly. It's all related to understanding the child in a way the adult would have wished to have been understood.

"I try to use experiences in my life that I either had or didn't have and bring it to fatherhood," Dwyane Wade said. "Right or wrong, that's the way I do it."

Wade, who won sole custody of his sons Zaire and Zion in 2011 and released the book *A Father First: How My Life Became Bigger Than Basketball* in 2012, spoke of basing his way of parenting on one simple principle: "I think you've got to know your kid, first of all. That is the most important thing, [knowing] if you have a sensitive kid or someone who can take criticism."

Zaire and Zion were born two years apart. They are little alike.

"My youngest son is the tough one," Wade said. "He's the tough cookie. So I understand that as he gets older he's going to be able to take things a little differently than Zaire, who takes things a little more emotionally. You've got to understand the personality. It's just like being on a team. Coach can't approach every guy the same. Everyone is a little different. Some guys can take 'in your face'; some guys need it to be positive and you pat them on the back. Same thing with kids."

How does Wade know?

"It's when you talk to them and whichever tone you are taking to them," Wade said. "You kind of look at them and you kind of read them to see how they are reacting to it. There's also watching them in certain situations. You know, when other people say certain things, you've just got to watch them. You've got to have open communication. The one thing I do try to have with my kids is open communication. Obviously no one ever wants to be in trouble. No kid ever wants to be punished. But you know what? If you've got to be punished, how would you want to be punished? Just ask them, just to see where their minds are and where they are going. I think you got to sit back, you got to watch, you got to look, and that's how you learn."

That's the attunement Wade wanted from elders as a child.

"That never happened," Wade said.

It did not happen while he was subject to an unstable situation and shuttled between his two parents, with his mother battling drug addiction before transforming her life.

That experience inspires him now.

"That was the one thing I said when I got older," said Wade, who was largely raised by his older sister Tragil. "I do understand being a kid. We do try to get over a lot of it thinking we're smarter than adults when we're young, but we're really not. But also I understand that it's not always what someone else says; it is neither. You know, I got in trouble a lot of times, and I'm like, it wasn't what they said but I got in trouble. So I do try to listen to my kids a little more and give them a little more leeway. Because I was a kid once, and I do understand adults. We're not always right. Sometimes we jump to conclusions right away. Sometimes it's not exactly what it seems all the time."

As his kids now make the jump to sports, Wade has come to understand not only how different they are but also how they respond to different voices. "I learned very early that my son [Zaire] takes it harder when I say something to him than when my brother [Demetrius, who trains Zaire] says something to him. If I say 'Zaire, I want you to do this,' he may not want to do it as quickly as when my brother starts teaching things."

This is even though Zaire's father is the one with an NBA Finals MVP award and two championship rings.

"I learned very early. I fell back, and I said, 'Okay, I'm just going to be supportive,'" Wade said. "And I will say certain things here and there. But I don't mind watching someone else correct his mistakes, because once they do that, I am able to come in and say 'Yeah, do you know why he said that, why they did that?' Then you become more of a second voice when it comes to basketball. But it's cool. It's fun to sit back. I told him the only reason he's playing basketball is if he's having fun and enjoying playing the game. So I enjoy watching him enjoy himself."

Doing so without saying a word is a form of communication in itself.

That's the technique that Malcolm Kerr, a Middle East studies expert and professor, usually used with his son. He would show up, without emitting much emotion through his voice or expressions. "My dad loved sports, but he was always quiet," said **Steve Kerr**, who spent many of his formative years learning basketball in Lebanon and other Arab states before spending his high school years in California. "He would go to every game and wouldn't say a word. He would support me without saying much, without saying anything. That's the best way to do it. Just be there for your kid. Don't yell at the ref. Don't question the coach's decision. Just be there to support your kid."

Malcolm never got to see his son play in the pros, where Steve won five NBA championships as a supporting member of the Bulls and Spurs. He was assassinated in Beirut while Steve was still at the University of Arizona. Still, Malcolm's early influence had an impact in many ways, including in youth sports.

"I got a great lesson there from my dad," Steve said.

Sometimes dads—and moms—can learn a lesson if they have an honest conversation with themselves. It can take some time to have, and heed, that conversation, especially if they expect a child to handle everything exactly as they did.

Tim Hardaway was toughened by his background, growing up on the south side of Chicago. As a collegian and a pro, even as he was taking and making big shots, he took plenty of criticism from peers, coaches, and adults. However, he made it work for him. "If you tell me I can't do something, then I am going to show you I can do it," Hardaway said. "I took the constructive criticism or negativity and turned it around to show you I could do it."

And so, as his son Tim Jr. was developing into quite a good player himself, Tim Sr. took the same approach that others had taken with him: he ordered, he complained, he criticized, and he didn't relent. But Hardaway's son didn't have the same disposition. Feeling stressed, Tim Jr. would get into arguments with his sisters, simply to take his frustrations out on someone other than his father. The tension and arguments spread and took over the household, with Tim Sr. often at odds with everyone.

"You want your kid to excel so much, in whatever they are doing, that it can break up or mess up a home or a household," Hardaway said. "Your wife gets mad, the other kids gets mad. Whoever you are fussing with, you are always telling them to do better. They get tired of hearing it."

Communication shuts down.

One day the former Warriors and Heat star decided to sit away from his family, far up in the bleachers, for one of Tim Jr.'s high school games. He saw the game and his own behavior from a different perspective. Hardaway's son team lost, but the Hardaway family gained something. Tim Sr. chose to reform. He apologized on the car ride home and promised more praise. That action proved to be as healthy for him as it was for his son.

"I am finding out just being a parent is much more exciting," said Hardaway, whose son would go on to star at the University of Michigan, before the New York Knicks drafted him in 2013. "It is much better for your child and your home. Just be a parent and support [your] kids in whatever they are doing, however they want to do it. I tell them they are doing a good job. If they ask me questions later, I will answer them. If they lose, I say, 'Try to do better.' If you win, I say, 'Don't rest on your laurels.'"

Hardaway's transformation and the space he gave his son brought them closer together. His son began to solicit more basketball advice. "I've got him right there, just twenty steps away from my room," Tim

Jr. told the *Miami Herald* while a senior in high school. "That's all I need."[9]

Hardaway's change was a major step for a family; one in which a father worked to rebuild a relationship by concentrating on building up—rather than breaking down—his son.

"Teach a Kid to Believe"

SHANNON MILLER sometimes felt invisible, and sometimes she wished she were.

She was so acutely shy as a young child that if she didn't know a person, she would hide behind silence. That's what made sports so unique and empowering for her. She didn't need to look anyone in the eye, or even open her mouth. She could speak with her skills.

"I could just perform," she said. "It helped my self-esteem. I was able to stay out of the traditional pitfalls of teenagers. Sports allowed me to be adventurous. I learned how to do things and that you just have to go for it."

Sports gave her purpose, validation and a voice.

"Now you can't shut me up," she said, laughing. "I would be a completely different person without sports. They gave me confidence."

Chipper Jones grew up in the tiny town of Pierson, Florida, where his father, a former Stetson University star and Chicago Cubs draft choice, was a teacher and coach at the high school. He was going to practices, playing catch, and swinging a bat from the age of three. As he got older, his mother, Lynne, a former equestrian star, let him bike between houses

---

9   Israel Gutierrez, "Tim Hardaway bonds with son on, off the court," *Miami Herald*, April 17, 2009.

miles apart to play pick-up games. Eventually he took part in organized leagues, from Little League to American Legion.

"I was an outdoorsy, athletic kid, and if I wasn't playing some kind of sport, I wasn't happy," Jones said.

His enjoyment was partly a result of his comfort of playing with kids he knew well. They were all different ages but from similar backgrounds. Then in ninth grade, Jones's parents sent him to board in the big city. He went to study and play baseball, basketball, and football at Bolles High in Jacksonville.

"I did not know anybody," he said. "I was a country boy amongst a bunch of rich kids; I did not fit in whatsoever," Jones said. "Until they saw me play football, until they saw me play baseball. All of a sudden I became Mr. Popular. To say that sports gives you an air of confidence and can lead to acceptability, that's an understatement. Athletic ability has a tendency to make you fit in real quick."

That's what it did for O. J. McDuffie as well.

"Sports made me more secure in my life, especially with relationships," McDuffie said. "It helped me a lot. I knew I could succeed."

Julie Foudy believed in herself from the start.

"I never had to deal with the issue of lacking confidence," Foudy said.

Her success in soccer only reinforced and strengthened her confidence. Julie's fascination with the sport began when she was just six. After kicking the ball around at recess, she told her mother that she "liked this thing called soccer." Could she sign up? Her mother made her wait a year. The wait, for Julie, was worth it.

Why did she like it so much?

"I liked being active, I think," she said. "I was really hyper and social. So it brought those two elements together. It was physically demanding and you were surrounded by teammates. I loved being competitive, and it kind of was an outlet for me where I wasn't looked upon as a freak. It wasn't that I had the overarching dream to play in the Olympics or the World Cup. It was truly because I loved being out there."

Julie loved playing, even when she was so small that her older brothers and older sister would, as she recalled with a laugh, "use me as a ball." She loved playing even though her search for inspiration was limited by her era and gender. She was born in California in 1971, the year before the enactment of Title IX, the ground-breaking legislation that would afford more equal opportunities to women at the high school and collegiate levels. The legislation positively impacted her later in her athletic ascent. But when she started, "there weren't the role models that you see today for women." While she followed sports, and was particularly keen on the Los Angeles Lakers, there was no women's national soccer team, no women's World Cup.

"There wasn't anyone I could look at it and say, 'I could be like her one day,'" Foudy said.

Still, that didn't stop Julie from making her own name. Summer after summer, year after year, she kept getting selected for more elite squads. Her confidence kept swelling.

Then at age sixteen she traveled to China with one of the women's national teams.

Suddenly, finally, she was shaken.

As Julie struggled against the skill of the other players on that trip, she started wondering "what the heck" she was doing there. "I was really insecure about it for a long time, trying to convince myself that I did belong there. So for the first time it was really hard. I had never gone through that. I had always been a starter."

What did she do?

"Just kept plugging away," Foudy said. "No particular breakthrough. I think eventually you just learn the techniques to help you become confident. I learned to channel my thoughts toward the positive rather than the doubts, which we all have. I learned over the years this is very normal. Butterflies are normal; we all have them. It is not something to get concerned about; rather it is a great thing. Just channel it in a positive way. But that does take a while. It took hard work while playing at that level to start to believe I belonged there."

As an adult, Julie Foudy eventually did more than belong. She became one of the most decorated female athletes of all-time, winning two gold medals and two World Cup championships with the US national women's soccer team. She reflects upon the China trip and her confidence slip as a critical step.

"It was interesting," Foudy said. "And it was great. Everyone needs to go through those periods of lacking confidence."

Everyone will, at some stage, in some situation—even the most advanced and talented. Boys as well as girls. Men as well as women.

That's the nature of sports.

It's also the nature of life.

Self-esteem, the sum total of beliefs and feelings that a child has about him or herself, is inherently fluid. That is because a variety of factors impact self-esteem, and many of *those* are fluid. Those factors include what a child receives in terms of love, support, and approval from the closest adults, as well as the way the child evaluates him or herself in terms of attributes and competencies when compared to the nearest peers. Those factors all fluctuate as a child grows and develops emotionally, mentally and physically, and through experiences at home, in school, and on the field.

Without question, sports, with their extreme highs and lows, can create both increased security and increased instability in a participant's self-esteem, and sometimes in the course of the same contest. This is especially true if the participant is young, impressionable, and inexperienced. It should be understood, as the Miller and Foudy stories exemplify, that not every child enters youth sports or an activity with the same reservoir of belief in oneself. Nor will every child develop that even after some success, or be equipped to maintain it upon encountering adversity. Even teens with healthy self-esteem levels can find their confidence weakened by new situations, such as joining a different squad, trying an unfamiliar sport, being moved to a new position, or encountering more advanced teammates or opponents.

How might a lack of self-esteem show itself? Kids with less inner security might not be open or willing to take the risk of trying anything out of their usual comfort zone for fear of falling short or facing ridicule. Instead, a child may retreat to preserve their personal worth. Some won't feel comfortable asking questions that would help them improve, either because they assume they are to blame for their struggle or they anticipate an unsympathetic or insensitive response. Some kids might just argue and refuse to listen to constructive advice, and some won't even see the point in practicing because they can't visualize any progress. If a child does try and still falters, he or she will only confirm and cement their lack of faith in themselves.

This is especially likely if they don't feel any external support.

So what can you do about it?

You can provide that support. You can infuse a child with the belief that he or she can accomplish something—and perhaps even have the power to make a dream real, no matter how unlikely that dream may seem.

"If you can teach a kid to believe in himself first and foremost, then the other stuff doesn't matter," Rollins said. "Teach a kid self-esteem first; that will go further than any coach or any parent screaming when they are giving instruction."

Or, as former Major League pitcher **David Wells** argued, "If you believe in your game, in your ability, you can take it to the next level and do that without anyone having to tell you otherwise."

But can you actively *teach* self-esteem? Can you compel someone to be confident?

Brandi Chastain argued that the process is one that is inherent in a healthy sports experience, which again is why she has welcomed girls' increased participation. "Young boys have been learning that lesson inadvertently," Chastain said. "They didn't say, 'Today, so-and-so boy, you are going to learn how to be confident.' Basically, they said, 'So-and-so boy, here is soccer. I am going to teach you the skills. The more you practice, the better you get. When that happens, you feel better.' Those were things young girls weren't [hearing]. And it is not that we are saying today we are going to build self-confidence or self-esteem. We are building you as a whole person, like young boys have been able to build themselves for a long time. And a byproduct of that is that [a girl] is going to feel good about the things they do, and that is going to carry over into other things in their life."

So perhaps "teaching" isn't the right term. It's a bit more involved than that. Rather, it's about exposing a child to an activity that will likely provide challenges but then facilitating their progress—carrying on an ongoing conversation that makes the child believe that he or she is valued and important regardless of the trouble that comes. It's about fortifying that child, but also educating and making the child understand that self-worth should not be tied solely to success in a sport.

"Your achievement can help your self-esteem, but it shouldn't be attached to any one thing you do, good or bad," said **Raul Ibanez**, a long-time Major League outfielder.

It is about making kids accept that while sports achievement has value, it won't, as Dwight Stephenson explained, "happen overnight. There's going to be some ups and downs. There are going to be some days you're going to go out and see some improvement; some days you are won't see any improvement. It doesn't come in big increments most of the time. It comes in little things. It's a process. Just be willing to stay the course."

If a child can come to understand that, he or she will be less likely to crumble when harshly questioned or unfairly criticized by others, no matter the circumstance or activity. Furthermore, a child will be more likely to weather the external storms in youth sports, whether they come in the form of incorrect calls, last-second losses, or individual disappointments. He or she might be more likely to weather the internal storms too, the doubts and frustrations that work on minds and gnaw on stomachs.

And most of all, they may be more likely to weather the fear, the emotion that most stifles dreams.

Even as an adult you know the power of fear.

You know how it can force you to stop in your tracks or veer off your course, anything to avoid experiencing whatever it is that you may dread. There are all sorts, levels, and origins of fears. What might frighten one person but not another? That is a consequence of many variables, from genetics to family environment to temperament to the interplay of each of those. Some fears start in childhood, while many are tied more directly to the adult experience. Some fears are shared by many, while others are more subtle and personal and the result of a previous negative situation that has left an indelible mark. The source of some fears can't even be clearly identified or understood. All fears, however, can elicit a feeling of vulnerability and helplessness for a person, unless the person can find a way to proactively use his or her mind to fight the fear rather than flee from it.

And there are plenty of good reasons for kids to be afraid of sports.

If you played a sport as a child, you may remember feeling anxious the first time you put on a uniform—or simply when you saw that uniform was lying on your dresser.

"I was nervous," NBA guard **Jamal Crawford** said of his early playing days, "especially before big games. You can't sleep the night before."

You may remember the edginess increasing whenever you trotted onto the field or court and saw eyes upon you. This happened way back when for NBA All-Star and champion Chris Bosh: "When people started actually being at the games, that got me nervous a little bit. There would be like fifty people in the gym, and I'd be like, 'Oh, it's packed!'"

If you played as a child, you may have been afraid of getting hurt by an opponent or by some instrument of the game, whether a ball, bat, stick, puck, or skate. You may remember feeling intimidated by the unknown, whether a new skill, play, coach or opponent.

You probably remember one fear above all: the fear of failure.

And you may hold that same fear for your own kids.

You just can't let it have a hold over you, or them.

"You Have to Have Failure"

Jimmy Rollins comes from an athletic family. His mother, Gyvonnie, was a competitive fast-pitch softball player. His brother Antwon played Minor League baseball. His sister Shay started for the University of San Francisco basketball team. His cousin Tony Tarasco roamed Major League outfields for several years.

Rollins has won a National League MVP, a World Series championship, and three Gold Gloves. Along the road, he has come to understand what every athlete eventually does.

"In every sport, there's a high percentage of failure," said Rollins. "Baseball, you're going to make plenty of outs. Basketball, you're going to miss plenty of shots."

That's the way sports are framed: for every winner there is a loser. In every situation there is a shot at success or failure, often in inverse relation for each side: touchdown or interception, goal or save, make or miss. In every game there's a risk that someone leaves the field of play feeling dejected, disillusioned, and inadequate.

It is not unusual for a participant, especially a child, to let one mistake overshadow the rest of an athletic performance. Nor is it unusual for children, who tend to view things as all or nothing, to let such singular sports failures define their overall worth—as if one strikeout means they aren't any good at anything at all.

As a parent predisposed to try to protect a child, you may be inclined to run from all this unpleasantness—all this, as Herm Edwards labeled it earlier, "inconvenience." You may see the potential adversities as reasons to limit the child's interest or participation.

The athletes we interviewed, however, would strongly advise otherwise. They would argue in favor of paving the path to resilience.

"How can you truly know what success is if you never experience failure?" former NFL quarterback Chad Pennington said.

"I learned far more in sports from losing than I ever did from winning," NBA legend Walt Frazier said. "Everybody loves you when you're winning. But when you lose, you have to come down, and you've got to regroup and come up from there. I guess that is the essence of sports: being able to handle the adversity and turn that into success. That's something you take into life."

Or, as former baseball star and manager **Joe Torre,** argued: "In order to succeed, to appreciate what you are doing, you *have* to have failure in there—so you know what feeling good is about, and why you feel good."

It's hard, however, for many kids and parents to see failure as a friend, especially when that friend can be so hurtful. Jay Feely, the long-time NFL kicker, bemoaned that "in general in our culture, we are afraid of failure." He also believed that, "if a kid can handle failure that is going to help them succeed. That will help them succeed more than anything else you can do for them."

That was the approach taken by Mary Joe Fernandez's tennis coach, the former doubles star Gardnar Mulloy. "His advice was, 'Put her in tournaments so she learns how to lose,'" Fernandez said. "And I lost every weekend. Learning how to lose at a young age is critical."

So is learning how to put something in perspective. That can take some time, but it's a lesson that can last a lifetime. "My favorite thing I tell people now when losing a tennis match, whether the Finals in Wimbledon or Finals of the State Championship, is that if that's the worst thing that happens to you, you've had a really good day," Fernandez said.

Heartbreak can even be the best possible thing for the long run. It gives a parent a chance to pose the question that long-time premier NBA defender Bruce Bowen does:

"Yeah, you want to win but you lost, so *now* what?"

It gives a child a chance to grasp the need for change and break old habits.

"You have to go through some failures to get to where you want to go, whether it is in school or sports," Pennington said. "We as parents have to focus on every once in a while letting our kids fail. We need to teach our kids not to accept failure but to embrace failure and use it as a teaching experience, use it to learn from."

John Smoltz didn't just embrace it. The pitcher chronicled it.

"My book that I wrote was about failure and how you can be great and better through failure," Smoltz said of *Starting and Closing*. "I always played in the top tournaments, the top games, and came up short. I had some tough games. But I learned most and best when I failed."

When he was fifteen, Smoltz was dominating his own age group in Michigan and felt he was ready to participate in a nineteen-and-under tournament in Johnstown, Pennsylvania. The scouts had their radar guns fixed on him. However, the ball kept flying faster the other way.

"Boom, boom, boom, boom," Smoltz said.

He gave up four two-run home runs—in the same inning.

"It radically changed how I thought," Smoltz said.

He went home and had a message for his father: "I need to work harder. I need to go to the next level."

And so Smoltz did, and he kept reaching higher and higher heights. Smoltz later looked back on that period as a "great time for me." It was the "start of a tremendous failure" that led him to a career that, after finishing as the only man with more than 200 wins and 150 saves, will likely be commemorated in Cooperstown.

As tremendous failures go, few in sports history can compete with what **Dan Jansen** endured and overcame over the course of his speed-skating career. He entered the 1988 Olympics in Calgary as a prohibitive favorite in both the five-hundred-meter and one-thousand-meter races. After learning that his sister died of leukemia, he fell in both events, even while holding a lead in the second one. However, he got back on his skates and set a world record in the five-hundred-meter race in 1991. He stood as the favorite in the same two Olympic events in Albertville, France in 1992.

He finished fourth in the five-hundred-meter race.

He finished twenty-sixth in the five-hundred-meter race.

He left empty-handed again, without a medal.

By the 1994 Olympics, Jansen had set four more world records in the five-hundred-meter race since his flop in 1992.

He finished eighth in the race this time.

There was just one shot left: the one-thousand-meter race.

What did he draw upon? The failures from his youth? From 1988? From 1992?

"I can't say there's one or two things, but I can say in general—I would say there was everything," Jansen said, laughing. "It was being the youngest of nine and getting beat all the time. Not physically of course! But when things didn't go my way on the ice, my dad always had a good way to keep perspective. It was like, this is tough, but this is life. I think a little bit of that is missing today for some. I think I am not a huge fan of getting trophies every time you play. It's not that I want kids to lose, but I think it is part of life. When you move on from sports into real life, you don't win all the time. It's the same thing. I learned everything from growing up in sports."

This includes the times he fell down.

And in 1994, he stood proud on the podium, after setting a world record, and taking a victory lap with his one-year-old daughter, Jane. He dedicated the gold medal to his late sister, and carried the United States flag at closing ceremonies.

Now he has a message to share with kids, and he does often.

"It definitely doesn't go your way all the time," Jansen said. "And sometimes it might not even ever go fully the way you want. But it comes down to the effort you put in and the journey you take, and the things you learn from it. When it's all said and done, those are all more important than whether you won or lost."

Like speed skating, gymnastics can be an all-or-nothing endeavor, particularly when you show the promise of a young Shannon Miller and everyone expects you to win. In one of Miller's early state gymnastics meets, she fell during her balance beam routine.

"I was devastated but I had to keep going, and I ended up winning the competition," Miller said. "For me that was a big deal, because it taught me that every moment counts. You can't just give up at the first sign of failure. Pick yourself up and minimize deductions."

That message stuck. When she fell off the balance beam again during the 1996 Olympic trials, she reached back to that earlier experience.

"This can be done," she told herself. "Get focused and don't make any more mistakes."

Jamal Mashburn's journey had some hard times as well.

"I had a bunch of failures," the former NBA All-Star said.

The one that hit hardest came when he was ten. His first sporting love had been baseball, but his environment wasn't exactly conducive—growing up in the New York City projects, nowhere near grass fields, with stickball often serving as an inadequate substitute.

He took a shot at the baseball team anyway.

"It was the first time I really tried out for anything," he said.

He got cut. That could have crushed him.

"But I was more self-aware than a lot of other kids," Mashburn said.

"I started to understand why I failed. It wasn't that I couldn't become a good baseball player. It was because I was unprepared for that style of baseball."

Jamal promised himself that he would not be unprepared for his next opportunity. After waiting three years, he tried out for the Gauchos, an Amateur Athletic Union team in basketball, a sport which was easier to perfect in the inner city. He made the team and two weeks later was playing in a tournament in St. Louis. Seven years later, he was in the NBA. Now he's a successful businessman, owning a real estate company and dozens of restaurant franchises.

"So I don't look at failure as a be-all and end-all," Mashburn said. "I look at it as learning experience. It tells a lot about who you are as a person."

Not every child, however, is as intuitive at a young age as Smoltz, Miller, and Mashburn were, able on their own to turn a disheartening experience into a teachable moment. Most children require the influence of another party: an adult. And most require a gentler voice than Jennifer Rodriguez heard. Even as a petite six-year-old, Jennifer was a tomboy, playing with GI Joes and worms while stuffing the dolls her mom bought in the closet. She sought outlets to express herself physically, and found the roller rink to be the place where she best fit in. But one particular day wasn't fun. She was speeding around the first corner when she took a spill. The tears started flowing. Her body wasn't moving, and her coach began yelling … and yelling, and yelling some more.

It seemed to her like it was "for thirty or forty minutes."

Rodriguez took it because she respected authority. And she felt even worse because she disappointed her parents as well, who always provided her with all the gear she needed.

"I never, ever lay on the floor ever again, no matter how bad I was hurt," said Rodriguez, who later won Olympic bronze for speed skating on ice. "That stuck with me. Everyone crashes and burns. Just get up and keep moving forward."

Yet adults should not take their cues from Rodriguez's coach.

"He scared the bejesus out of me," Rodriguez said.

It is better in most cases to support rather than to scare, especially after failure puts kids in a fragile state.

At age eight, Sanya Richards-Ross was racing against girls a year older.

"I was really, really small," she recalled.

Still, she ran really, really fast, fast enough to place second in the sixty-yard dash.

But since it wasn't first, it felt like last.

"I thought the world had come to an end," she said. "I was crying on the podium. It was tough. My mom and dad told me it was okay. The next year, I went on to be a champion girl for the next class. That moment had inspired me to work hard. It also humbled me. It let me know that others work too. But you keep working, and you can be a champion. When you lose, you think your parents might be mad at you, and you are ashamed. But when they are proud of you anyway, they pick you up and hug you, and they are equally proud of you, that's an important lesson that you learn—that it's okay."

For Sanya, losing was a start, not an end.

"We have to be there to encourage kids through the failure," Chad Pennington said. "We are there to make sure they are not harmed and not put in danger. We can't fix all their problems, but as long as they stay safe, we can help them through the failure and the experience."

You must make kids understand that no one wins all the time, not even their seemingly indestructible sports heroes. After all, they don't. No one ever escapes the chance of failure and the concerns about it entirely. The athletes that you, and your kids, may respect or admire have come up short too many times to count.

Shane Battier was always an advanced athlete, so much so that he not only won the Michigan state championship for the Punt, Pass, and Kick youth football skills competition, but also set records doing so.

"I had a rocket arm," Battier said, smiling. "I was *good*."

In 1990, he was twelve and competing in a PPK regional championship (with Michigan, Indiana, Ohio, and Illinois) at the old Pontiac Silverdome, prior to an NFL game between the Bears and Battier's team, the Lions. His first punt was perfect.

"Then I shanked the kick," he said. "I was a toe kicker. I put my toe on it, and like a lot of toe kickers, it came off my foot wrong and I got five yards."

The passing competition was still to come at halftime.

"But I knew I wasn't going to win," Battier said. "I was devastated. I literally ran up to the stands where my parents were, and I was crying. I felt so bad. This was not a team sport, but I felt I had let myself down."

And in front of more than fifty thousand, including those who mattered most.

"I look back and laugh at it, but at the time, it was tough," said Battier, who has won championships in college and the NBA. "I wanted to win."

Certainly, he didn't set out to humiliate himself, but it happens. To everyone.

In his NBA career, **Chris Mullin** would score 6,740 baskets in the regular season alone, not including 3,616 free throws and not including those made in the playoffs or while a member of the 1992 Dream Team. You may remember many of the Olympic shots that counted for his team. However, you may not know what happened in fourth grade.

"I scored on the wrong basket," Mullin said. "It was embarrassing. I was wondering why I was so wide open."

Even when wide open as a pro, as one of the masters of his craft, he missed 7,503 times from the field and 562 times from the line.

He still earned a spot in the Basketball Hall of Fame.

Michael Jordan, arguably the greatest NBA player in history, said in the iconic Nike commercial: "I've missed more than nine thousand shots in my career." By the time he retired for good, Jordan had missed 12,345.

"I've lost almost three hundred games," Jordan continued on to say in the commercial. "Twenty-six times I've been trusted to take the game-winning shot and missed. I've failed over and over and over again in my life. And that is why I succeed."

The relationship between failure and success goes both ways. As failures can lead to future success, past success can help even the youngest athlete through failures.

"Success in the past is what you always reflect on, because you know that you can do it, you know you've gotten it done before," O.J. McDuffie said. "So when you hit a bump in the road, you think about some of the good things that you've already accomplished and you try to live off of that."

This is important to remember because, in sports, the potential for failure and the tension related to it never entirely vanish. It merely needs to be managed.

After rising from fifth-round draft pick to seven-time Pro Bowl selection, **Zach Thomas** still dealt with inner turmoil: "I had a fear of failing. I used it as motivation sometimes." He tried to harness it so that it would make him step back and reflect but not stop him cold.

Thomas never appeared afraid to compete, and certainly neither did Jordan. Of course, at a certain point they also had track records of extreme accomplishment that helped them shake off any failures and not let it hold them back from the next opportunity. They had plenty of experience dealing with the glare of a spotlight and the harshness that comes with it.

The average child is not nearly so immune to uncomfortable feelings in the presence of what they perceive as pressure. For many, performing can be petrifying. That's because the fear is about more than just the disappointment and pain resulting from the potential of a poor individual performance or team defeat. It is also, at its heart, about the fear of losing another's approval, interest, admiration, or even love. This explains why NFL All-Pro tight end **Jason Witten** put so much pressure on himself at age eleven when his grandfather, a high school football coach, showed up to watch him play. "I was scared to death. I didn't want to mess up. I remember that feeling."

In an extreme form, that fear of rejection by others can lead to a rejection of oneself, which then interferes with one's ability to continue or improve. In some cases, the extreme apprehension will be clearly apparent through a temper tantrum, a refusal to participate, or a complaint about a physical symptom such as a queasy stomach. The child may not share any feelings in order to avoid disappointing the adult whose approval is sought.

There are two primary types of performance anxiety, one enduring and one temporary, their differences again speaking to the differences between different children. Some children have a trait orientation and are prewired to worry about how they will do and how others will react. This is independent from but can be exacerbated by state orientation, in which the alarm arises from the specific pressure-generating moment or event, such as the final inning of a championship contest. In either case, the anxiety can disrupt preparation and affect the action, changing what the child's mind and body can and will do.

Sometimes the anxiety creates inaction.

At age thirteen, Chipper Jones felt the pressure. He was competing in an All-Star state championship game in Sarasota, Florida. His team was trailing by one with the bases loaded, two outs, and a full count. Even at that age and that stage, he was counted upon to play like a star.

"I was expected to come through in that situation," Jones said.

The pitch came straight down the middle.

His opportunity.

"I froze," Jones said.

Strike three. Game over. Dreams dashed—in a blur.

"I just wish I had swung the bat, at least given us the chance," Jones said.

Chipper's father, Larry Sr., was the team's third base coach, with a clear view from just ninety feet away. Larry Sr. didn't yell, either in public or private, like Jennifer Rodriguez's coach did. He told his son to shake it off, not because he meant to artificially pump him up or because he believed that taking the pitch was the right move, the umpire had made the wrong call, or the outcome didn't matter to anyone who was playing or watching. Rather, his purpose was to lend perspective, perspective that came from his knowledge of the nature of the game and all the factors required for success in any particular situation. So he reminded Chipper that anyone who played long enough, no matter their ability, would have many such moments—moments of failure.

Moments that, after such a jarring event, a thirteen-year-old might fear facing again.

Moments that are so common that one future Braves teammate, Brian Jordan, experienced nearly the same disappointment as a child, but at an even younger and more vulnerable age. Jordan was seven when he failed to come through in the clutch.

"I cried my eyeballs out because I felt like a failure," Jordan recalled.

Same as Jones had.

"I think I cried about it for days," Jones said.

Still, both would appreciate their respective fathers' comfort for years. Earlier we wrote of fortifying a child's self-esteem so he or she can better endure adversity. In these cases just mentioned, the fathers fortified their sons through their failures, with the clear understanding that no single failure should ever define any child.

"My dad said, 'Look, did you play your hardest? Did you give it your all?'" Jordan said. "I said yes. He was like, 'That's all you can do. Baseball is a game of failure. You are going to fail more than you succeed.'"

Both athletes would even come to appreciate, rather than lament, their early setbacks, understanding what needed improvement and making the necessary adjustments to realize their potential.

"Learning experience," Jordan said.

"Learning experience," Jones said.

Did both later encounter failure as their fathers forecasted? Of course they did and plenty of it—as individuals and as part of teams, even while Jones was winning a World Series and an MVP award and Jordan was pulling the rare double of starring in the NFL and the Major Leagues.

But they never stopped swinging—figuratively and literally.

"It was that one situation in my life where I was like, if I ever get the opportunity again, I am not going to stand there with the bat on my shoulders," Jones said. "I will say this, there have been a couple of years when I have ended the season in a playoff game."

He smiled.

"But I didn't strike out."

An early, unforgettable failure became Jones's fuel, as he went on to accomplish much individually and collectively. Even in the final at-bat of his career, after an exemplary individual season, Jones made sure the bat didn't stay stuck on his shoulder. With two outs and two strikes in the bottom of the ninth in the wild card playoff game against St. Louis, he put the ball in play, reaching on an infield single.

Tom Glavine also went on to accomplish much after early exposure to what most kids encounter: contests or competitions in which they perform to their capability individually but come up short collectively. It isn't necessarily a negative for a child to be concerned about the group result rather than merely his own contribution; in fact, as we mentioned earlier, selflessness, commitment to the team, and accountability are virtues that adults should most want kids to build through the youth sports experience.

So it was hardly a strike against Tom's character that he hated to lose. He hated to lose even at the youngest age, whether the sport back in Boston was baseball or hockey or anything else. That was a feeling he never lost as he got older and he became a three-hundred-game winner in Major League Baseball and a candidate for the Hall of Fame.

"Back then we didn't live in an age where you'd get a trophy just for playing," Glavine said. "And I think that was the greatest life lesson for me. That was the one thing I carried with me to this day from my childhood that served me well."

His competitiveness served his growth as a person rather than stunting it, because, with some help, he learned how to harness it.

That help came from Tom's father, Fred.

"I remember my dad telling me early on, 'Look, you're going to walk into that locker room with a smile on your face, and you better come out of it with a smile on your face or I'm not taking you anymore,'" Glavine said. "And I've always remembered that. And that's kind of what I try to do with my own kids. It's all right to be mad when you don't win, but don't lose the enjoyment of what you're doing based on the outcome of the game."

But sports taught Tom more than just one lesson.

He learned to set a goal and passionately pursue it—to play as hard and as well as he possibly could, applying the skills he had honed during practice for the purpose of achieving a victory that he could share with others. He learned to be relied upon by peers while also relying upon them. He learned to participate rather than simply observe, to expose himself to the possibility and pain of failure. He learned to take an activity so seriously that it upset him greatly when he didn't succeed.

And Tom also learned, through the guidance of his father, how to modulate all of that—how to handle a situation when his best, or the best of those around him, was simply not good enough that particular day. His father didn't ignore his sore feelings; Fred acknowledged Tom's frustration and anger. But it was also made clear to Tom that he was better served channeling his emotions in a constructive way than letting them overwhelm him, undermine his performance, and keep him from moving forward. It was made clear that losing didn't make Tom or any of his teammates "losers."

Through organized youth sports, he learned about disappointment. Through that, he learned about acceptance. He learned how to let something go and keep going. He learned skills and virtues that would be invaluable no matter what path he chose in life.

Does any of that sound like failure?

SECTION 3:
Why Limits Matter

"A Delicate Balance"

JULIE FOUDY is not merely a champion in sports, she is a champion *of* them. The former US women's soccer team captain is a proponent of so much of what sports can provide to young people, especially its role in the cultivation of a competitive spirit—and especially in girls. She knows how difficult it is for many girls "to come to grips with being competitive" in a society that reserves those expectations for boys. She knows the challenge for girls in finding the balance between going for the gusto and "oh, you don't want to do that to your friend." She knows that she wouldn't have wanted her competitive instincts squashed. Those instincts were always strong. While bouncing the ball on the asphalt in fifth grade, Julie could hear a teacher speaking to her mother, marveling about Julie's determination in every endeavor. Her mother agreed and said that she hoped Julie stayed that way, especially since Julie's older brothers had been a bit more of a challenge to motivate. "I wanted to be very successful in school," Foudy recalled. "I wanted to be a good athlete. I don't know where it came from, but I'm glad I had it!"

Yet, now, as an adult observing other adults' behavior, she's *had* enough.

She's had enough of the current climate in which adults apply intense and pervasive competitive pressure, pressures that can extend beyond the field or court, or even any single game or season.

She's had enough of the parents who fret that a daughter no more than six years old isn't spending every bit of spare time doing squats in the weight room, and when she asks if the daughter even likes soccer, they say they're not sure.

"Maybe you should find something she really likes," Foudy replies.

She's had enough of the parents, coaches, and club directors passing on so many of the pressures *they* feel to the kids—pressure to start earlier than a child may be ready. Pressure to get into elite programs before anyone else.

Pressure to pour all of the focus and attention into a single sport. Pressure to play that sport year-round, every waking minute. Pressure not only to win every time but to be the person most responsible for the victory. Pressure that feeds upon pressure. Pressure that never stops.

Pressure that dwarfs what was present when Foudy was growing up.

"It is so different," Foudy said. "If you talk to any of the gals who I played with on the team—Mia [Hamm], Brandi [Chastain], Christie [Rampone], [Kristine] Lilly—we all grew up in a different era, when you could play a variety of different sports. There wasn't the end game you have today."

In her recollection, kids were playing more for "holistic reasons." They were playing more for their own reasons.

"These kids are signing contracts at the age of seven or eight," Foudy said. "It is different, it is a lot more intense. We had a club team that was awesome, and our entire radius where people [in the program] lived was probably ten to fifteen miles. Now you have people driving three times per week, two hours each way, to get to training. You are putting pressure on kids to perform in a way that does not help their development. I think it hinders their development. And it is a pay-to-play system now. The coach [of a high-level team] is someone who could be making five, six figures per year. It is now about winning because his livelihood depends on it, whereas my coach was just a dad and I thought he was great. He was not going to get fired. He did not have to worry about putting food on the table for his family [through coaching]. I think there is less time to develop kids, and it is more about results."

The ESPN analyst decided to invest her own time in an attempt to start reversing the trend. The Julie Foudy Sports Leadership Academy, an annual, six-day residential retreat for girls aged twelve to eighteen, devotes half of its energy to soccer and half to a leadership curriculum.

"I thought too much emphasis was on results and headlines, the wrong things in sports, and that parents and all of us were kind of losing sight of the fact that the real beauty of sports is that it completely defines who you are," Foudy said. "It gives you confidence, your self-esteem. There isn't a day that goes by—and I've been retired since the 2004 Olympics—when I don't call on something I learned from playing or from a teammate, or that I learned from adversity and loss. All these beautiful things you learn from sports. And I don't think that is just because I played at the level I played at."

Through her academy, Foudy tries to shift the obsession from getting a child to play at that sort of level—an Olympic or professional level—and "put the focus back on the true value and gift of sport." Rather than keeping score by who tops the scoring chart, she wants to help the girls set other goals.

"I think there are so many opportunities to learn about you by just participating, which is especially important for girls in finding their voices and becoming stronger women," Foudy said. "To be okay with who you are, to understand that we don't have to all look the same or be the same—that is okay. You can be different and that is good. That is the message I want to get across for girls. I hope you can use sports to

[reel] them in but then use sports as a vehicle to teach the girls that we all can lead."

But what about the adults? How is their leadership improved? How is the runaway pressure train stopped?

We can start by acknowledging this:

"I think parents are put in a really hard spot," Foudy said.

Without question, they are forced to make lots of hard choices. Many of them manage to make plenty of the right ones, and make it a more pleasant experience for all others involved. Penny Hardaway returned to Lester Middle School in Memphis for the 2011-12 middle school season and thoroughly enjoyed leading that team to the West Tennessee State title. He didn't find the parents to be a problem. If he struggled with anything, it was with the kids and their "little attitudes," the sixth, seventh, and eighth graders who "want to play but don't want to practice, don't want to run. They don't want to do the hard stuff. They just want to play games."

The parents, however, served as a source of support for him.

"I walked into a great situation," Hardaway said. "But usually the parents are tough as well."

They can be, even if they don't mean to be.

Parents can easily fall prey to projection. From the past, they can project their own unfulfilled dreams and ambitions on the child, perhaps without even fully realizing it—as fallout from a conscious or even subconscious lingering feeling that they fell short of their own athletic potential when roughly the same age. They can fall prey to the hope and desire that a child gets closer to glory, fame, and wealth through sports than they did. This can lead to the projection, into the future, of unreasonable accomplishments for the child, expectations that may result in part from surface knowledge of the success story of some exceptional athlete. After all, if Eldrick "Tiger" Woods was putting in front of Bob Hope and Mike Douglas while a preemie, and eventually became a champion, why can't their own offspring start along that same course? Why can't their son or daughter reach such heights, and lift them into the spotlight by association?

Former soccer star Brandi Chastain, a member of the National Advisory Board for the Positive Coaching Alliance, sees this sort of distorted mindset manifest itself all the time: "I think when you look around and see all the athletes who make millions of dollars, it's hard for a parent not get caught up in something like; 'That could be my child.'"

And that could be *me* with them, a parent might think.

Jeff Foster, who recently retired after thirteen seasons with the NBA's Indiana Pacers, excuses parents for simply reacting to all the current conditions, even if he doesn't agree with their actions. "I think with the money nowadays, that's a driving factor," Foster said. "When I was growing up in the 1980s, sports weren't at the forefront of everyone's mind from a career standpoint. Now, obviously, the salaries are so great and the exposure is there; you have a chance to be a global figure. I don't blame them. Parents want their kids to be doctors and lawyers, and now athletes make more money than all of those people."

He adds: "But hopefully they don't push [kids] too hard."

Or too soon. Again, that gets back to the Tiger tale.

"You watch sports now and parents are so focused on trying to create this robo-athlete," NFL kicker Jay Feely said. "You don't have to decide at six years old what sport they are going to be professional in, which is what it seems like a lot of parents do these days."

Some parents are earnestly trying to do something else: they are trying to do the right thing for a child.

If you bought this book, you are undoubtedly one of those parents, grandparents, uncles, coaches, or mentors. Yet you still may be tempted to take the "early, intensive, exclusive" approaches that many accomplished athletes discourage.

Perhaps you think a certain athletic activity will be good for a child, even if the child has resisted or others don't believe the child is ready. Perhaps you see the child finding tremendous and extended joy in a particular sport, and you think that more and more exposure to that sport will give the child even greater pleasure. Perhaps you see promise or potential while watching a child in a particular activity, some sort of exceptional ability that that is obvious not only to you but also to those around you. Perhaps you have some guilt about your lack of availability due to work or other family responsibilities, and so you wish to compensate by providing expensive equipment, individualized instruction, and constant competition; in this sense, the sport helps to entertain the child while introducing another adult support system. Perhaps you live in a football hotbed like Florida and have come to the same conclusion that former NFL player **Oronde Gadsden** has while living there. Gadsden, who didn't play organized tackle football until college, chose to expose his son Oronde at age nine.

"It's Florida, bro," Gadsden said. "You think you are going put your kid in next year at ten, but the kids from the park, who have been playing since they were been six, they're hitting. They're squaring up, their head on the right side; they're grabbing; they're driving—boom! Your kid's going to be like, 'I can't breathe.' For real. If we were in Minnesota, you could play at ten. It's just, we're in *Florida*. Everybody's kid is playing early because they think they have a chance."

Perhaps you are in Minnesota, and you see the same thing happening in hockey that happens in Florida with football, baseball, and soccer. Perhaps you see what former NBA player Steve Kerr does all over the modern sports landscape, even if he deems the resulting obsession and immersion a shame: "If you aren't playing year-round, you fall behind the kids who are."

Perhaps you want your kid to stay even or get ahead, simply so he or she has every opportunity to gain positive lessons from sports way down the line.

Perhaps all of your impatience and persistence comes from the most selfless, redeeming possible place.

"I don't fault the parents for loving their kids," Chastain said. "But what they need is to be educated about how to support kids in a way that allows the kids to enjoy the game, and then they become better."

What you need to understand is that, whatever your intentions, the effect of a pressurized, all-consuming focus on a single activity can be just as detrimental.

You need to understand the existence of limits.

Leading a child toward sports? That's often good. Pushing a child toward sports? That's more problematic.

Showing a child how he or she can do something better? That can work well. Screaming at him or her to do it, or else? Forcing him or her to do it differently than the coach is instructing? Those things can be destructive.

Being active around and invested in a child's team? Naturally, that's your responsibility and your role. Meddling in everything? That is to be avoided.

Encouraging a child to work toward winning? That's part of what makes sports great. Tying the worth of the experience entirely to what the scoreboard says? Everybody loses when that happens.

Giving a child the best chance to succeed at the sport in which he or she shows the most initial interest or aptitude? That in itself is not a bad thing either.

But, again, there should be limits.

If there's pressure, it should be on you, the one guiding a child, to work toward respecting those limits.

"First and foremost, parents need to realize there is a very, very fine and delicate line between encouraging and pushing your kid," said Cheryl Miller, one of the greatest women's basketball players of all time. "And it's a delicate balance for parents who are eager, especially sports parents."

In this section of the book, we deal with all those fine lines, lines over which it's easy to trip:

The fine line of initiation between the child wanting to play and the adult pushing the child out there.

The fine line of supervision between an adult showing up and showing interest and failing to show the necessary understanding, restraint, and etiquette.

The fine line of competition between a healthy emphasis on collective goal-setting and improvement and an excessive emphasis on winning at all costs.

The fine line of specialization between a concentrated effort in one endeavor and an obsession that excludes the exposure to—and experience of—anything else.

The fine line between helping and hurting.

"Left up to Me"

DERRICK BROOKS saw one practice.

He saw enough.

He was a Pensacola kid, just seven, and this was his first day of football. He didn't find any of it all that appealing.

"I turned my stuff in right after practice," Brooks said. "I told my dad I was not going to play."

The person he told was not his biological father, whom Derrick wouldn't meet until several years later. Rather, it was A. J. Mitchell, the man who had recently married his mother, Gerri, the man of the house. Mitchell was a disciplinarian, believing strongly in respecting authority, even if that authority was not him. Mitchell believed that so strongly that three years later he stormed into a fifth-grade classroom unannounced, saw Derrick acting out, and taught the boy a lesson about being a class clown.

"Right there in front of the class, he tore his belt off and tore my butt off," Brooks said, laughing. "His messages were very simple: You are going to learn how to treat people. You are not going to be a very disrespectful young man. No matter what you do in life, you are always going to respect people. That was the last time my father put a belt on me. I got the message. I started treating people the way I wanted to be treated. That has been my life motto."

You might think that someone so stern would have reacted poorly to Derrick's decision to pass on football so quickly. You might even assume he went back to that belt. A. J. Mitchell's belief in respect, however, carried over to the way he treated his stepson. He respected Derrick enough to listen. He respected Derrick's wishes enough to say this, and to mean this: "Son, if you don't want to play, you don't have to."

So Derrick didn't. Not right away. When baseball started, the same peers who had played football were out on the diamond. They encouraged him to pick up that pastime.

"I enjoyed baseball a little bit better," Brooks said. "Then when football rolled around, I thought I'd try again. My parents never stressed to me that I had to play sports. They gave me the opportunity to do what I wanted to do; then they just made sure I had fun doing it."

Brooks eventually did everything at a high level, whether in the classroom (graduating Washington High with a 3.97 GPA) or on the field (winning a spot on the Florida High School Athletic Association's All-Century Team). After a brilliant football career at Florida State University, where he also earned an advanced degree, he made eleven Pro Bowls and won a Super Bowl with the Tampa Bay Buccaneers before retiring in 2008. He earned the respect of players, coaches, fans, media, and prominent community figures; that admiration embodied by his receiving the NFL Man of the Year award in 2000, the NFL Defensive Player of the Year award in 2002 and a place on the FSU Board of Trustees in 2003. And eventually that respect for Brooks, who is now a television and radio analyst, will extend to induction in the Pro Football Hall of Fame.

Would Brooks have accomplished all of that if he had been pushed? If his stepfather had ordered him to get back on the football field the very next day? If his stepfather had embarrassed him in front of peers, demanding that the coach make it easier for his son? If he had felt the pressure to enjoy and embrace the game immediately? If he hadn't been allowed to come around on his own, finding the fun rather than being forced?

"Let kids be kids," Brooks said.

That's what A. J. Mitchell did. He understood that this kid, like so many kids, needed to make his own choice on his own time. So he let it go. He let it happen naturally. He let Derrick initiate.

You might assume that Brooks represents an exception and that many of the athletes we interviewed would have had a different experience. They all "made it" in athletics beyond the average person's wildest dreams, not just grabbing spots on professional rosters or Olympic teams but excelling after doing so. Someone *had* to have pushed them at the beginning and along the path, correct? Otherwise, how could it have happened?

Those assumptions couldn't be more incorrect. Almost uniformly the athletes have said they had to find their own way.

"I did not have any pressure from my home," David Eckstein reflected. "I did not have any pressure from my coaches."

"My parents were always like, 'Whatever you want to play, fine; I'll take you,'" Tom Glavine recalled. "If you don't, that's fine too."

"My parents were supportive, but I was always self-driven," Shane Battier remembered. "I never had anyone tell me to go to the gym and practice."

Keith Sims did, but at least he was sufficiently comfortable that the person making the suggestions had his best interests in mind. He didn't enjoy football as a high school freshman, and he wasn't planning on trying again. Then a new coach begged him to give it another go.

"I went out, and after one week, I started as the tackle on the varsity team," he said. "I loved it."

He loved it and he pursued it—for himself.

It is always better if the kids make these choices, about whether to play and what to play. Some of the choices will come later in the development chain, as we will cover in the chapter on the risks and rewards of specialization. But here's one example: Juanita Brown, a single mother and full-time nurse, had encouraged her children, including **Rashard Lewis**, to stay active, through organizations such as the YMCA, so that they wouldn't be idle and so they might use sports as a means to fund the furthering of their education. Rashard loved football most, but he was growing fast—six inches after eighth grade—and the basketball coach told him he could join varsity if he gave up the gridiron. He was upset, and torn. "I wanted to play football *so* bad," Lewis said. He sought direction from his mother, as he always had, and—even as a proven veteran in the NBA with a couple of All-Star appearances to his name—he still does. She told him that he she couldn't pick the spot for him. He needed to make the call. He needed to take his time, take everything into consideration and then take action. He chose to pursue his promise in basketball rather than his passion of football. His later success proved that he chose wisely.

But so had she, by letting him take initiative and ownership.

That is the best way for it to happen.

Pushing isn't merely unhealthy, it is often unproductive.

It can, and probably will, backfire.

We've made it clear throughout the book that if your goal is to turn your child into a professional athlete, you would be wise—given the extreme longshot nature of that—to reassess your goal. And if your plan to beat those odds is to relentlessly push your child, you would also be wise to reassess that approach.

"My husband [surfer Laird Hamilton] and I will never be that," Gabby Reece said of parents living vicariously through children. "First of all, it doesn't work. Both of us have similar experiences, different formats, where it was *our* thing. That's the only way it works. If you have love for something, are passionate for something, there's nothing that can replace that."

In the absence of that initial passion, parental pressure can be even more detrimental, preempting any possibility of the activity slowly growing on the child.

"If you force anything on your child," Alonzo Mourning cautioned, "you'll make them hate it."

"He might turn off," former basketball star Walt Frazier said.

If pushed, your child might never turn onto an activity, the way that Reece's stepdaughter Bela did. Initially Bela told Gabby she had no interest in sports. Gabby left it at that. Bella changed her mind, joined Gabby for underwater pool training, and quickly proved to be the "best female" Gabby had ever trained in anything.

Quentin Richardson never needed to be convinced to head out to a basketball court.

Nor did anyone try to nudge him.

"It was left up to me," Richardson said.

It was left up to Richardson to join a team during his adolescence, and it was up to him to work on his game, on his own or with family and friends, when he got home. It was left up to him after his interest "clicked on," and he started receiving awards and accolades for his abilities, to decide that "maybe I can do this." It was left up to him after he struggled in an Adidas camp after ninth grade to prepare better for the Nike camp the next summer.

"It was because *I* was motivated," Richardson said. "Not because I came back and my pops, my coach, or anybody were like, 'You didn't do good enough, so now you've got to do this.' It was never that. It was just that I was hungry enough, and so I went and did it."

So what if Lee Richardson and the other adults in Quentin's life had treated him the way that he sees so many treating today's kids:

getting "too serious and too intense too early," voicing their primary, and seemingly solitary, message that "you've got to be the best," and putting the sport above all else at all times?

What if they acted like the adults at the camps he sponsors back in Chicago?

After all, Richardson's had to tell those adults things like, "Yo, these drills are too advanced for them. What are you doing? We're not trying to make an Isiah Thomas out here. They're six. They can't *do* all of that yet. Just let them go. Just put them on the court, and keep them away from the big kids. Just let them go."

How would he have felt as one of those kids around such adults?

"That I don't know," said Richardson, who has played twelve NBA seasons. "I see kids like that who don't like it. And they don't like the sport anymore. And that's not for everybody that it always happens that way. So I don't know because it didn't happen to me. I don't know how I would have been affected."

Richardson knows what worked for him. It's what worked for so many of the athletes we encountered—the influence and guidance of adults who followed the formula stated by Richardson:

"Be cool. It's not cool when you force things on kids that age. At a certain age, you can turn that on but, early on let the kids enjoy the game."

You can expose a young athlete to more advanced assignments and establish greater goals over time. But even as the athlete moves into his or her teens, the emphasis on their enjoyment should not be entirely sacrificed. There's no justification for making a young athlete—or those trying to instruct the young athlete—miserable and turning an activity he or she once anticipated and adored into something to despise and dread. Unfortunately in this respect, too many adults lose patience and perspective, and the youth sports experience can take a turn for the worse for all involved. If you recognize any of your own behavior in some of the stories shared in the next chapter, you should certainly take pause.

"Shut Up and Clap"

FOR JASON Taylor, it's been a blast.

"Priceless," Taylor said.

What could possibly be more fun and fulfilling for a parent, especially when one in the latter stages of their own football career, than watching a son enjoy the sport they adore, while serving as an active participant in their development? That's what the former Dolphins standout has done with his sons Isaiah and Mason, in leagues close to his home in upscale Weston, Florida. He moves up divisions as they do, with the skill level and strategy getting more advanced at every stage. Taylor played for seven head coaches in the NFL, some he liked and respected more than others. Now he's a coach himself, albeit with much younger pupils, players who are still pulling flags rather than making tackles.

"The on-the-field stuff ... I love every minute of it," Taylor said.

Off the field?

"You deal with some parents."

Actually, he deals with them on the other sideline too—the parents with the whistles in their mouths, the clipboards in their hands, and many kids under their care. He deals with the parents who are also the coaches.

"The other coaches have been the disappointment: their desire to beat me and talk trash and be unsportsmanlike," Taylor said. "I've coached against teams whose coaches have yelled and dropped the F-bomb on a seven- or eight-year-old. It's unbelievable."

Taylor jokes about it with his wife, Katina—these adults taking kids' flag football so seriously. But some of it hasn't been so funny. In one game,

Isaiah intercepted a pass, and two opposing coaches got so heated and vulgar that Taylor took his own team off the field.

Taylor's experience has confirmed his long-held belief that parents should be seen in the crowd and not necessarily heard.

"I think the same thing goes for parents and coaches—to an extent," Taylor said. "Shut up and clap. Just shut up and clap. Let them have fun. They are not going to be pros. They are not going to make every play. Heck, we are paid to do it and we don't do it."

As a coach, Taylor savors the success of a particular play, especially if it's one he designed, taught, called, and then watched executed to perfection.

"But I will also high-five a kid when he makes a mistake," said Taylor, who is now an ESPN analyst. "The yelling, the screaming, the 'What were you thinking?' ... well sometimes you need a pat on the back. The kid is getting instruction on the field but doesn't need it on the sidelines, doesn't need it in the car. The worst thing for a kid is to see disappointment on a parent's face."

He's tried to avoid showing that to his own sons. When Mason was distraught over throwing an interception in Taylor's flag football camp, Taylor told him that all the quarterbacks Mason loves—Tom Brady, Peyton Manning, family friend Dan Marino—had thrown lots of interceptions.

"It's not about that pass," Taylor said. "It's about the next one."

While coaching baseball, basketball, and football, former Major League outfielder and NFL safety Brian Jordan has encountered plenty of parents who don't understand that, especially in basketball. As soon as he starts sensing trouble, he lays down the law. He tells them: "I got this. Leave your kid alone. I don't want to hear you screaming his name during the game. Talk to him when he gets home."

This is not always easily accepted.

"The sad thing about sports today is that every parent, [after] their failures, is trying to make their kid live out their [own] dream," Jordan said. "And I get frustrated when I see a parent yelling at a kid because the kid is not successful on the field."

Grandparents do it too. Once Jordan grew weary and angry with one grandmother who kept berating her grandson for not moving faster.

"Finally I just went over to her, and I said, 'Grandma, I got this. You are not helping him by screaming at him,'" said Jordan, who continued encouraging the boy and watched him get in shape as the season progressed.

Such unreasonable expectations exist even in what many would assume to be the sweetest, most innocent stages of sports. Just ask former NFL star **Rodney Harrison**, who started coaching his sons Christian and Rodney Jr. in T-ball when they were five years old and worked with older groups as they aged. "The problem with parents in youth sports is that most of them think their kid is very good," Harrison said. "They think (their kid is) going to get a scholarship or be the next Major Leaguer. It just won't happen. A lot of times the parent wants their kid to be the pitcher, wants him to be the quarterback, the star running back."

Harrison addresses parents prior to each season and tells them that his intention is teach their kids the fundamentals as well as teamwork, sportsmanship, discipline, and the respect for authority. But he also makes it clear that while the kids will learn plenty just being part of a team, it doesn't mean every kid will have the same role. "We are always going to make the decisions to make our team better," Harrison tells them. "Bottom line."

That means everybody.

"I am fair," Harrison said. "If my son goes out there and doesn't play well, he's not going to play. He's not going to be a starter."

Oronde Gadsden didn't initially intend to coach his own son, Oronde Jr., but when the former NFL receiver tired of others instructing inadequately, he decided to step up and take the reins of a tackle football team composed of players no older than nine and no heavier than ninety-five pounds. Over time he has taken some other steps in order to exert some control and avoid parental anarchy. He imposed a rule that he won't talk with parents about that weekend's game until the next practice, usually on a Tuesday.

The rule isn't often obeyed, not even after a win. He gathers his players in the food and water tent and tells them to give themselves a hand. They scream "Yeah!" He reminds them of the game next week and that they "can't do new stuff if you don't come out to practice." He speaks of the need for corrections and then asks the other coaches if they have anything to add. After they share, he breaks the meeting down with a "1-2-3" and a "see you on Tuesday."

That's meant for everyone.

But as soon as he says the number "3," before his daughter can hug him, he can help his son remove shoulder pads, or he can even get out from under the tent, "there's parents."

In his face.

"They get their kids and they are right at you, like, 'Hey, Anthony didn't play today," Gadsden said. "And I'm like, 'Hey, the only day we talk about these things is Tuesday.'"

There's logic behind that.

"If we lose and I'm upset about losing, and you come to me talking about how your kid didn't play, I might not be in the right frame of mind. You might not be in the right frame of mind," Gadsden said. "S--- is going to be bad. Out there, in front of people … you don't want that."

But around the nation, coaches get that.

David Wells wanted to give something back to the community where he got his start, a community that appreciated him enough to name a field after him. He was a starting pitcher on the last Point Loma High baseball team which won a California Interscholastic Federation championship in 1982. Nearly two decades later, after a Major League career in which he won 239 games, including a perfect game, Wells returned to serve as the pitching coach. His pupils are much older and more advanced than those under Harrison's and Gadsden's supervisions. Their parents, however, may be even more problematic.

"You got to keep the parents out of it, because they're the ones that just keep screwing things up," Wells said. "They are e-mailing, they are complaining, and all that. They weren't doing that when I was coming up."

That was true even though Wells had an unusual childhood, as the son of a single parent who associated with Hell's Angels. The bikers would attend his youth games and pay him for strikeouts and wins. While we're not endorsing a financial method of inspiration, at least the bikers' hearts were in the right place. They didn't barge in. They kept the appropriate distance, and they didn't become distractions.

"Just go there and support, you know?" Wells said. "And leave it up to us to work with them and develop them. And if a kid is a freshman, he's got three years to do it. You just can't be antsy unless a kid is a standout."

In his first season back with Point Loma, Wells became disgusted with one parent of a pitcher who was posting social media criticism about the head coach and the team.

"Why would you do that?" Wells wondered. "Because your kid isn't playing every game, you're going to try to sabotage the program? And this is high school. To me that's just preposterous. But to each their own. They are just ruining it for the kids, basically, because when you get a parent who is like that, it really reflects on the kid. Now the manager is pissed off, and he's not going to play him. Just to be spiteful, a lot of people would do that. I want to play the kids. I want to develop every one of them."

Wells sent out an e-mail blast to the parents of all the pitchers, offering to open his door to any who had concerns or complaints. "Not one person called me, but they still bitched to the head coach," Wells said. "I said, 'Send them my way. If they do it, send me their e-mail, and then I'll reply to it.'"

If **Brett Hull** had coached youth hockey players rather than simply watching his son Jade compete in the sport, he likely wouldn't have been so tolerant as Wells or Smoltz. The Hall of Famer, who scored 741 goals during his NHL career, got annoyed enough just watching the coaches. "You go and watch your kids practice, and they teach them no skill. The art of making plays with skills is gone. I hate it."

The parents? His views on many of them would make ice melt. "I would tell parents to go away," Hull said. "Parents are the worst things that have happened to youth sports. They shouldn't be allowed at the rink. First of all, they are standing up there and they are yelling. They have no idea what they are yelling about. And then it's like, 'My kid doesn't play enough.' Well, your kid doesn't play enough because he's not good enough. I mean, face the facts."

Hull's sharp opinions aside, our intention here is not for parents to hit the curb, simply for them to curb their bad behavior, which can come in many forms. "One thing that is hard is when you have parents who cheer when another child makes mistakes," Mary Joe Fernandez said. "Really, you are cheering for a double fault? Come on."

"It is disappointing sometimes," said Major League pitcher Tim Hudson, who has three school-aged children in sports. "Also, it makes me kind of chuckle. For the most part, man, I think when you get into the competitive leagues it is out of control. You get the parents who do have some sense, who actually have an idea about life; they understand this is a kid's game. When you put too much pressure on kids, it's time you need to look yourself in the mirror and realize you are an idiot."

When a mirror isn't available, a muzzle might do. Sometimes it helps for parents to hear the sweet sound of silence. The latter is what many youth leagues have done, ordering all spectators and coaches to zip their lips, even if it's for just for one day each season. That "holiday" called Silent Saturday has spread from basketball to soccer (with the endorsement of the American Youth Soccer Organization) and across the country. The idea, according to AYSO promotional materials, is to "just let the kids play and have fun without having to worry about how their performance is affecting the adults on the sidelines." Additionally, the intention is to help "the few parents and coaches who feel they must provide constant direction understand how disruptive is it" and "to show all parents that the kids can play well on their own with limited instruction." Kids may even play better since they can actually hear each other.

However, parents sometimes have a hard time accepting that a child can succeed without them, no matter that child's age. Karrie Webb has observed much more of this "helicoptering" dynamic on the Ladies Professional Golf Association tour, even when it concerns competitors who are in their twenties. "Parents have become a lot more involved," Webb said. "I was a rookie sixteen years ago, and there were no parents out on tour. Now they are everywhere. The parents fall in love with the tour as much as the kids do, and they never leave. They stay out there as long as the kids do. And their kids don't grow as people, not even counting how they are as athletes. And when they rely on people too much, it doesn't allow their talent to really bloom."

Again none of this means parents must completely stay away. As we emphasized earlier, showing up and showing interest are critical elements of the youth sports experience; doing so shows a child that you care, and that helps foster the trust in you and in themselves that will serve them well as they grow. It also shows a coach that you are making sure he's setting the right example.

"My dad was real rah-rah; my mom was real rah-rah," said Cheryl Miller, whose younger brother Reggie was also a star basketball player. "But parents in the stands, standing up and yelling at the coach? Make sure you are the best sports person for your child to model after."

When you cross the line, you undermine a child's chances of reaping many of the benefits of youth sports—the principles Harrison is trying to instill in the kids he coaches, including discipline, respect, dignity, and cooperation. What message is the child getting when the adults are exhibiting so few of those qualities themselves in their own interactions, whether with children, other parents, coaches or even officials?

"You have to teach them the right values for camaraderie," said **Jeremy Roenick**, one of the all-time great American hockey players. "You've got to teach the kids the right sportsmanship for having good integrity. Unfortunately, what happens—and I think it is epidemic everywhere—with hockey is caused by the refereeing and the way the refereeing is. It is so totally atrocious that the fans, parents, and everybody get all get riled up. Then there becomes that lack of respect and that lack of integrity."

That possible pitfall isn't isolated to hockey. Officiating can rankle participants and spectators of every sport. But you, as an adult, have to rise above that so you don't drag your kids down into it.

Mike Miller, who sank seven three-pointers with an aching back to help the Heat win the 2012 NBA championship, has sons who play baseball and other sports. He also sponsors traveling AAU basketball teams. Miller sees the youth sports world as "far more advanced than when we were in it." He thinks there is a trend toward parents having much more personal investment rather than investment for their kids. This manifests itself not only in pushing the kids to try to perform but also in pushing the limits of good taste and behavior. "The fights and arguments between coaches and parents, parents and parents ... to me that is an embarrassment," Miller said. "It takes away from the kids having fun and enjoying it."

It can take away from the enjoyment of a game when an adult publicly challenges every play, call, or score that doesn't go one child or team's way.

While Andre Ware singled out fathers for this sort of behavior, the reality is that many mothers also treat their kids, and other adults, in a way they likely wouldn't wish to be treated.

"It drives me crazy," Dan Jansen said, "when you get the know-it-all parents. Most of the coaches are volunteers. They are giving up their time, and then you've got the parents yelling at them. It's embarrassing, also for their kids. I can't imagine doing that to my child. I've also seen the kids when their parents are yelling and screaming and the kids are sitting there with their head down; you see they are not real proud of what's going on. It's a bad situation."

Especially because, as John Smoltz noted from watching his own kids, much of the noise is nonsense.

"Why do you never say a word when you come to the games?" parents would ask him.

Smoltz's answer?

"Because everybody else is doing things that are so embarrassing," Smoltz said. "And I know the kids are trying their best. But you're yelling encouragements that are just discouragements to kids. You go to a Little League game, and you hear, 'Keep your eye on the ball! Get the ball down!' You know if the kid could do it, they would do it."

Goose Gossage closed many games during his Hall of Fame career. When watching his own kids play, he wishes many spectators would close their traps.

"You can hardly stand to listen to these parents," Gossage scoffed. "*Every* kid's a big league pitcher. Every life's lesson is out there on that baseball field, and whether they make it the big leagues or not is not going to be up to you as a parent."

That's not to say parents are powerless about everything. Naturally, they're not.

"You can support them," Gossage said.

He cited one way: teaching kids respect for others, including opponents. This is an element of sportsmanship Gossage believes has been lost in baseball, from Little League to the Show. It has been replaced by braggadocio and showmanship.

But there are many, many ways to support kids, as we have noted throughout the book. There's simply a distinction between supporting and, in figurative terms, shoving.

"Parents, let your kids grow into what they need to be," said **David Robinson**, a Basketball Hall of Famer. "The only things we need to be focused on is making sure they're getting their academics together and their priorities straight. We teach them habits. That is the best thing we can do as parents. We can't put our dreams on them. We cannot make them be something that they don't need to be."

And yet, as NBA player Elton Brand has observed, "the parents, their goals, they kind of get lost on the kids, which isn't fair."

Most of those goals are extremely unrealistic, viewed through the rosiest of glasses. Too many parents lose sight of reality, focusing on results over process, focusing on the individual over the group, putting undue pressure on a child. That's not fair. Nor is it fair to a child when another adult essential to a positive youth sports experience—the coach—frames every athletic experience only through an all-or-nothing prism of winning.

"Winning Isn't Everything"

Joe Namath accomplished plenty during his NFL career, on and off the field, earning the nickname "Broadway Joe" and captivating a city and country with his charm and arm. He is no doubt best known, however, for what he did in 1969 after a heckler challenged him at the Miami Touchdown Club in advance of Super Bowl III.

"We're going to win Sunday," Namath blurted out. "I guarantee it."

The Jets did win, with a score of 16-7 over the favored Colts, and changed pro football forever.

Roughly a quarter of a century later, Namath was a dugout father for his daughter Jessica's softball team when a nine-year-old girl approached.

"Hey, Mr. Namath, we don't have to win today," she said. "We're just here to have fun."

In his Southern drawl, the former Jets quarterback had a ready response, a different sort of guarantee.

"You know what, honey? You are right," he told her. "I can promise you one thing: you are right but we will always have more fun winning than not." No one can deny that. Everybody has more fun when their youth team wins—kids, parents, and coaches.

Few would argue there's anything inherently wrong with competition with oneself or with another. Sports wouldn't be sports without it. The stark scoreboard framework, separating winners from losers in unequivocal and inarguable terms, allows participants to know exactly where they stand on a given day. Winning, Namath noted, should be gratifying; and losing, as Herm Edwards eloquently explained earlier in his dissertation on "inconvenience" and resilience, should be instructive and motivating.

Edwards, of course, famously said something else that warrants referencing here. In 2002 while coaching the 2-5 Jets, the New York media insinuated that he should stop worrying about the results of the present, and start planning instead to develop the team for future seasons. "This is what the greatest thing about sports is," Edwards replied, shaking his head then leaning over the podium. "You play to *win* the game!" Then he paused and called upon his hands for emphasis. "Hello!" Edwards said. "You play to win the game! You don't play to just play it!"

Edwards's team won eight of its next ten games, including a first-round playoff contest. The catchphrase, "You play to win the game," became Edwards's signature, and even the title of his 2004 leadership book.

Edwards seemed an appropriate person to ask for his views on winning at all levels. In high school sports, Edwards surmised, "It becomes pretty important to win."

Before high school?

"I think the emphasis on winning is maybe a little bit over the top at a certain age," Edwards said.

Others think so too—plenty of others.

"I think there's so much emphasis that's being put on winning and not development," former Major League pitcher Jamie Moyer said. "And when I say development, I'm not saying development for a sport; I'm just saying development as a person, mentally and physically."

That emphasis can be way over the top for the kids who already come to the field or court with shaky self-esteem. Pressure to win, to please another or to gain acceptance can escalate a child's anxiety, inducing a tentative, poor performance in that moment. It can cause even greater inhibitions when encountering similar situations in the future. Alternatively, other kids may lash out angrily as they cannot swallow their disappointment.

This raises questions: At what age is the average child prepared to pivot from youth sports focused on participation to those more centered on competition? When will a child be fully equipped to handle the "inconvenience" and disappointment that comes with playing in leagues or on teams that assign wins, losses, statistics, praise, and blame to everything, and for coaches who manage their teams in that manner?

To these questions, there aren't universally correct answers because there is no average child. Every child is a unique individual.

"I don't think there's a magic number," Moyer said. "Say you live in the inner city versus the country, you're dealing with two different animals. You're dealing with maybe two different types of opportunities. I think you just get a feel for it. Instead of forcing things to happen, you just allow them to happen. And I think you read your children. You communicate with your children and just say, 'Hey, how are you liking the opportunity? Let's have fun with it.'"

With his five kids, two of whom are now playing college baseball, Moyer's strategy has been to wait to start that communication in the car ride home. "I try to ask questions, try to get feedback from them, try to get feelings from them," Moyer said. "To get an understanding of what they're sending and what they're feeling. And what their experience is, and if I can add to it, I will. What are they experiencing? I try to let it be their experience, because you know, my experience was completely different."

As a father and flag football coach, Jason Taylor has come to understand the differences in development in relation to handling winning and losing. "It's tough to put an age on it. It probably depends on the child."

It does. Some kids may be more inclined than others—due to athletic, intellectual or psychological capabilities—to embrace the pressure of competition. Some kids may be more equipped than others to handle the consequences of that competition, including the criticism that can result from an individual struggle or a collective defeat. Some kids may be inclined and equipped at the start. Some may be late bloomers.

"My oldest son, Isaiah, was competitive from the day he came out," Taylor said.

Isaiah was so competitive he made his grandmother's wish come true. Georgia Taylor always told Jason that she hoped someday he ended up with a son that was as much "a pain in the butt" as Jason was, in terms of wanting to win at everything.

"If he loses, he's just like his dad," Taylor said, laughing. "Everything is a competition. If he's riding in the car with me, and my wife, Katina, is with the other kids, we have to beat them home."

Taylor's second son, Mason, was more happy-go-lucky while competing. His reaction when his father would tell him to run the ball? "Whatever, Dad."

By the time Mason turned eight, Taylor noticed that "it's getting more serious for him now. He's getting to the point where he has some dog in him."

You need to understand your own child's competition threshold, and specifically the child's tolerance for losing, so you can recognize whether a particular sport, program, or coach is appropriate for that particular child. You should be aware that not every sport is the same when it comes to the competitive expectations and burdens; some of them come with competition embedded from the onset but aren't truly competitive until higher levels when others are paying more attention to the outcome.

Dan Jansen, as a speed skater, was "already competing, literally, when I got on skates at age four. It wasn't like you won or lost today; it was like you *raced*. Though ten or eleven is when I started to think about kids in my age group and beating them."

Some individual sports, such as tennis and swimming, give kids a ranking against peers well before they reach puberty. Many team-oriented sports are far more structured, especially at the younger age levels, with national and local organizations establishing rules and encouraging their coaches to delay the competitive aspects and put a premium on something other than the score.

In the previous chapter, we introduced you to one of the undeniable crises of youth sports: parents who, governed by their own misguided ambition rather than the desires of the child, display inappropriate bleacher behavior. Are some of those adults interested in whether the team as a whole wins or loses? Sure. That's often what gets them cheering or booing. But it's not always the score that rouses them to rip officials, coaches, or other parents. It's how one player—their player—is faring. Many are really fanatical about a single individual, consumed by the concern that their Jimmy or Mary will somehow be wronged even if the team wins. Wronged by not getting innings. Wronged by not getting passes. Wronged by not getting shots. Wronged by not getting a chance to give someone else—notably themselves—a shot at reflected glory.

For coaches, the score may matter more. The problem is that sometimes it can matter so much that nothing else does. Youth coaches can lose perspective about their place and come to believe what the Vince Lombardi famously declared about sports: "Winning isn't everything, it's the only thing." The coaches may believe that that statement applies to them as much as it did Lombardi's Packers, and if that requires the same sort of screaming and scolding, so be it. They may shirk their responsibility to serve as mentors and guides, obsessing instead on padding a record and résumé in the hope of getting the right person's attention, and perhaps even vaulting to the next coaching rung. They may fail to recognize the critical distinction between molding highly impressionable children and driving highly compensated adults.

Shannon Sharpe shakes his head as he sees that play out regularly on youth fields – coaches trapped in fantasy, fancying themselves as Bill Belichick or Tom Coughlin, conducting NFL-style training camps, bullying and berating kids as if they are Tom Brady or Eli Manning and mature and motivated enough to endure any indignity.

"You're forty years old," said Sharpe, now a CBS analyst. "You've got the kids out there doing wind sprints and pushups. Don't live your life through them."

Youth coaches may give in to misguided ambition, just as parents do.

"When we were competing, you never saw the coaches arguing back and forth," Rodney Harrison said. "Now coaches get mad. They're screaming; they've got all different types of communication devices; they are watching tape. It's crazy. These kids are seven, eight years old."

The problem is too many current coaches don't see kids as kids. They see the kids as pawns, as means to *their* end. That's how you end up with stories like the one in September 2012 on The Today Show and CNN, reporting on allegations that coaches of a California Pop Warner football team paying ten and eleven year old players to hit opponents as hard as they can, which is the same sort of behavior that led to significant suspensions against the NFL's New Orleans Saints.

"When I was nine, ten years old, I felt that it was free," NBA guard **Kevin Martin** said. "You had fun. Now I look at nine, ten years old and they're getting cussed out by the head coaches and their parents. It is a lot more competitive than it was when I started to play competitive sports."

It only gets more competitive at higher levels.

After retiring from the NFL, Bennie Blades became a high school football coach, hoping to make the same sort of developmental difference for others that his own youth coach, Johnny Alexander, made for him. He couldn't stomach what he saw. For other coaches, it was all about winning, and any coach who didn't follow suit was viewed as falling behind. So Blades gave up coaching for refereeing, thinking he could have more impact that way and at least help kids learn to respect rules.

Coaches?

"It's about themselves," Blades said. "I hope to get into coaching once again one day, when things turn around and it's not about 'me, I'm the coach, I'm 14-0,' but about the child. How many athletes have they produced that went on to college from high school? You [think] you're successful. But isn't the point about the *kids* being successful? That's the legacy you want to leave behind. It is not about your individual record."

Some coaches would just as soon not focus on their record. They simply feel they have little choice because of the way too many parents behave. They're not necessarily thinking of getting ahead. These coaches are thinking merely of avoiding headaches. Oronde Gadsden is not trying to make his name in coaching. He already made his name as an athlete in South Florida as a popular longtime member of the Miami Dolphins. But while coaching his nine-year-old son's football team, Gadsden came to the conclusion that winning is an absolute necessity.

"Trust me when I tell you kids have a better time if they win," Gadsden said. Just as Namath had told his daughter's friend.

But Gadsden added something else from his experience, something that points directly to the twisted priorities of some parents.

"If they lose then you start losing kids," Gadsden said.

He'll ask why "little Johnny" isn't coming to practice, and he'll hear that Johnny just isn't having fun.

Gadsden knows what that means. "Cause they ain't winning."

It's enough of a hassle for Gadsden to get parents, and their kids, to commit to the team in all the necessary ways—an investment that requires more than showing up for the fun stuff. Many parents nag him about the number and length of practices. They come up with excuses to justify their children's absence from those practices—too long a ride or it's raining where we are—and then they demand to know why their child spends game days watching from the sidelines.

"If you're winning, you can say, 'You need to bring your kid,'" Gadsden said. "That's that *only* fight you've got. It's just the reality of it. It's easier for you."

And to that end, Gadsden has essentially decided that he can't play players "who can't help me win." Of his twenty-four players, half had never played before this season. Three, including his son and his former Dolphins teammate Sam Madison's son, far outclass their teammates in experience and ability. His message to them is simple: "You ready? You're not coming off the field." They're his cornerbacks, running backs, and wide receivers. They even run down on kickoffs. In his view, there's nothing wrong with the lopsided distribution of playing time.

"The parent is like, 'It ain't all about winning; I thought it was about playing,'" Gadsden said. "Well, as long they're taking score ..."

Gadsden's story, which touches upon the way that a parent and coach can impact each other, and not always for the betterment of the child, leads us to one of the longest-running and most contentious debates in youth sports, another one that requires careful consideration:

Who gets to play and for how long?

"The Best Possible Position"

COACHES HAVE the power to make decisions not just about one individual, as a parent does, but about the entire team. Some put the emphasis on the developmental interests of the greatest number of participants. Some put the premium on winning. Some have good reasons for doing one or the other. Some don't.

The best you can hope is that coaches are inclined to give their actions serious thought, and that they attempt to proceed to act appropriately for the kids they are coaching.

While coaching his sons in flag football, Jason Taylor has taken this approach: "I let every kid play, every kid run the ball. As they get older, you try to win." Taylor has gone so far as to "bribe" girls on his team to run with the ball, simply because he wants *everyone* to play some role. Perhaps this is a product of Taylor knowing too well the feeling of being left out. When Taylor started playing sports as a kid in Pennsylvania, "the biggest thing for me was the 'not getting picked' part."

Yes, there was a day when no one wanted Jason Taylor on their team. There were actually many days. And yes, he was wounded every time. "I would be one of the first ten guys there," Taylor said. "They would wait until eleven showed up."

When he was playing AAU basketball, he was left to wonder: "Why am I never getting a chance to get off the bench?"

Eventually he did get in the game, but he always suspected that his mother had worked on the coach to give him a shot.

"It was always the nonacceptance that drove me to work harder," Taylor said.

Certainly that is the case for some kids. Others, however, are adversely affected by such an experience, whether it is comes during unstructured pickup games, when peers choose the teams and starters, or during organized events in which adults are responsible for divvying up roles and playing time. Coaches can become so obsessed with results that they fail to think, or care, about the emotional impact that approach is having on those not viewed as valuable to their victory chase. Furthermore, coaches may not realize, or care, that by showing favoritism to more advanced athletes in other ways, they are making the others feel inferior and insecure. That can lead the less favored to a range of negative reactions, from sadness to anger to apathy, as well as resentment toward peers and/or authority figures. Ultimately this dynamic can foster distrust, disharmony, and dissension on a team, which certainly does little to help the cause of winning, if that was the coach's original and overriding objective.

"I would tell a coach or a leader of a team the same thing I would tell a parent: put kids in the best possible position for them to succeed," David Robinson said. "They have strengths and weaknesses and not everyone is a superstar. But everybody has some role they can play. Put them in a position they can be good at. We need to spend more time on our strengths than our weaknesses, so we can find our place. I think that is the best we can do for our kids."

Mark Spitz, the Olympic champion swimmer, coached his kids in AYSO soccer. He appreciated and enforced the rule that kids play three out of every four quarters.

"I think the nature of that edict in the sport provides an opportunity for people to feel good about themselves and participate," Spitz said.

While those kids were participating, Spitz made sure to hold them accountable for their effort.

"And those kids who *are* really good have a sense of responsibility to make sure, and are encouraged to uphold, that the team doesn't lose," Spitz said.

It should be acknowledged that some athletes we interviewed did not endorse the equality mandates that they see at some levels of youth sports. They believe there is greater value in standards, setbacks and measuring sticks; Mark Jackson spoke to this in an earlier chapter, when he recalled his childhood desire for more playing time as the impetus for putting in more practice time. Tom Glavine spoke against everybody getting a trophy. Brett Hull belittled parents who moan because their kids don't play enough, when the real problem may be that their kids aren't "good enough." Andre Ware believes "everyone that participates should get in the game at some point," yet challenges the conceit that "everyone has to win."

"We sometimes tend to pamper too much," Ware said. "In Texas, where I am, four teams go to the playoffs and districts, some with losing records. That needs to stop."

Former NFL linebacker Zach Thomas also chafed at the "nobody loses" approach to athletics, if it artificially levels the playing field, eliminates peer comparison, lessens motivation, and doesn't allow for the development of determination and resilience.

"Because when they get out in real life, after high school, it's not that way," Thomas said. "Yes, as a young kid, you are going to cry. In some physical education classes, they're jumping rope with no rope, so everyone wins. That's not how tough it is out there in society. If you don't learn early when you are eighteen and nineteen, and then get out in the real world, you are going to have problems."

From the get-go, Thomas got beat, got up, got in more practice, and got better. "You learn to win, and see how good it is," Thomas said. "You strive to keep working to get the best out of yourself."

There's certainly something to be said for rewarding the best players with the most trophies and nicest compliments. Those awards and accolades can serve as motivating factors for that child or teenager or perhaps even another; it brings focus and passion to an activity in the hope that practice will pay off. Still, there's also something to be said for limits, and at times, for a softer, more inclusive style that doesn't leave anyone far behind, even those less directly instrumental in winning.

Some coaches fall into the trap, however, of trying only a top-down approach: counting on a couple of kids to lift the entire squad rather than building up those on the bottom to make it easier on those stars. Worse, some coaches will excuse poor behavior from a player who is putting up numbers on the field or court.

"At that level, there's going to be better players," said Jamal Crawford, a Sixth Man of the Year winner in the NBA. "Some kids will advance a little faster than others."

Even while Crawford quickly became one of those better players, he appreciated that his coaches didn't play favorites.

"They cared about everybody," Crawford said. "And I think kids can feel that. They know if the star is treated differently than the guy who's not playing. And that's the part that stuck with me, because I remember coaches who treated everybody the same. If somebody got something special then everybody did. There were no special privileges."

As a coach, Brian Jordan has felt pressure from the parents of the most athletically gifted kids to cater only to their children. "Parents will always struggle," Jordan said. "Their kid is this great athletic kid, but you want to teach him how to be a complete player, especially at a young age—how to be a team player, a leader. And parents don't get that. 'My kid should score every basket.' I don't want him to score every basket. I want to make sure the next guy can score."

That is not just for development purposes either.

It is for a better chance at winning.

"Come playoffs, come championship, I need these other kids to learn along the way," Jordan said. "[The star] is going to be double-teamed, triple-teamed, I want him to be a leader."

That sounds like a good thing to be, at least when you listen to LeBron James. When James won his third MVP award, this one in 2012 while playing for Miami, he called his Heat teammates onto the stage to share the moment with him and to thank them for their sacrifices. He spoke about how "individual accolades come with team success" and how he learned early how the happiness of the whole could help him.

He learned from an adult who set the right example.

"I'm all about team," James said. "It's all I care about; it's all I know. When I first started playing basketball, I played in an eight-to-ten league. It was called the Summer Lake Hornets; it was a rec league and we had five games. We went 5-0, and I felt like I was the best player on the team. At nine years old you can't tell me I'm not the best player on the team. But our coach, Frank Walker Sr., who was also one of my mentors, gave the whole team MVP trophies. Everybody. Not just me. And right then and there, I knew it was bigger than just me. This game is all about team."

When a coach makes winning bigger than anything, that coach might do more than recognize and reward one player over another; he or she might overburden that star player emotionally or even physically, in the expectation that the player do everything necessary to achieve victory. This is acceptable at the professional level; during the Heat's 2012 and 2013 championship runs, coach Erik Spoelstra put plenty on James's broad shoulders, asking James to bring up the ball, bang in the post, defend all five positions, and rarely, if ever, take a rest. But James was twenty-seven years old, a grown man with a fully developed body (six feet, eight inches and a muscular 250 pounds). It's much different and far more dangerous to make similar physical demands of an adolescent who may not be emotionally mature enough to handle the pressure and, worse yet, is far from grown into his frame.

David Wells's youngest son, Lars is named after the drummer of Metallica. Not surprisingly, he has taken an interest in music. Yet Lars also plays baseball, and he has started tinkering with a curve at age thirteen.

"He's got a pretty damn good one," Wells said.

Yet Wells, who threw an excellent curveball during his playing days, has pumped the brakes a bit during Lars' development.

"You don't want kids throwing curveballs at ten and eleven years old," he said.

Curveballs can put plenty of strain on an elbow or shoulder, young or old, but especially young.

"They need to develop," Wells said. "They need to learn how to do it. If [a kid] is taught properly how to find that release point, you can start them at fifteen or sixteen years old. But do it correctly. And you're good to go."

Wells makes sure that, if Lars uses it, he's using the right mechanics. He does the same thing with the older kids he is supervising as a high school pitching instructor. Of course, many coaches aren't nearly as qualified as David Wells to teach those mechanics. Yet, in their desire to give their teams more tools to win, they may rush a child to add something to the pitch repertoire before taking the time to show how it should be safely done, or to find the expert who can.

An overemphasis on winning can bring out the worst in coaches in another way: they can abdicate their responsibility to emphasize and promote fair play, which is how you end up with allegations like those mentioned in the previous chapter, about paying pre-teen players for the hardest possible football hits. When parents also are fixated on the score or standings rather than sportsmanship, kids may adopt a similar attitude and feel liberated, empowered, or even compelled to find ways to bend the rules. As we noted earlier in the book, many kids don't need much cause to cheat a little; they can summon a variety of excuses for doing so.

So what's a winning strategy for a parent when some of the circumstances, as shown in this chapter and the previous chapter, play out? When winning has become everything? When a kid is suffering from being pushed, or ignored, by a coach?

A parent's initial protective impulse might be to pull the child out of the situation. That may become necessary, but it's hardly the only option.

Kurt Warner, the future Hall of Fame quarterback, has two school-aged sons who are five years apart, both of whom share his fondness for football. He views youth sports as an opportunity for them to learn leadership from those on teams and those coaching them. "Sometimes you learn it from people who display it and sometimes from people who *don't* display it," Warner said. "I raised my kids in such a way that in any situation they are going to be able to determine if that's good leadership or bad leadership. There is a bunch of garbage that goes on in youth football. We had a skirmish between coaches in a game, and it was ugly. But my kids, they learn what not to do. 'That's not how you respond. I won't ever do that.' They have to have the character to respond favorably to every situation."

Even at the professional level, Warner didn't agree with the decisions or styles of every coach.

"But you have a choice on how you can deal with it," Warner said. "You don't avoid situations to teach things. I don't know if you're going to have a bad coach or a good coach, but I know there's something you will learn from both sides, so let's learn it. Let's learn it and let's apply it in life. What can I learn from this?"

The parent taking this approach must do plenty of learning of his or her own; becoming fully informed is critical to determine how to appropriately respond. This requires seeking answers to a number of questions through the investigation and observation of the coach and communication with a child.

What is the coach's history, training, and experience? Is the coach promoting team building by honoring and respecting differences, setting realistic group goals, and encouraging collective involvement? Or is the coach playing favorites? Does the coach solicit ideas and hear concerns from everyone or just a few? Is the coach leading through inspiration or directing through fear?

And, especially, is it clear that the coach is putting winning in its proper place, or is there evidence that the coach is fixated on victory at any and all costs?

From reading this book, you may have even more questions now.

Didn't we argue that a parent should refrain from contradicting a coach's words and methods in most cases, in order to avoid giving the child unjustified reasons to disrespect the coach's authority? Yes. Didn't we caution against parental intrusion that comes from a lack of perspective in the form of constant ranting, raving, and complaining? Yes, that too.

Still, there *is* a place for a parent in certain situations to prevent a coach from injuring a child emotionally or physically. There is a right for a parent to act as a child's advocate and try to rein in the reckless coach on a quest for personal glory.

"As a parent you have to pay attention to a kid's coach and his style," Trace Armstrong said.

It's critical to carefully monitor the way a coach's interaction, communication, and approach, whether by actions, words, or gestures, are affecting a child. A parent may feel the need to pick up a child who feels beaten down, perhaps because the child is not getting an equal opportunity to contribute to winning or is being scapegoated by a coach or teammate for contributing to a loss.

"You have to act as a balance," Armstrong said. "You have to temper the hard blows. And there are other times when kids need to know what is right, and the parents need to provide some discipline. They need to let the kids know why something is important. If the coaches don't do it, then the parents need to do it."

By asking of the aforementioned questions, the parent can determine how to put the coach's behavior into perspective for a child. The parent should not try to make the case that winning doesn't matter at all; most children wouldn't believe that any more than they would believe the parent can fix it by magically creating the outcome. In the words of former volleyball star Gabby Reece, a parent should try to serve as a "figure of constant support."

"You don't freak out if they win, like, 'That's my son!' You don't freak out if they lose and be like, 'Why did you do that?!' That's the only way you can set the tone—if you are always the constant support figure. Otherwise, there's no winning."

In that way, your steadiness can serve as a counterbalance to an unpredictable or even unprincipled coach. You can remind the child that, no matter what anyone else says, nobody wins all the time, no single player is entirely responsible for a defeat, and not every factor is within a competitor's control. You can praise a good effort even if it didn't lead to a good result. You can do this by starting with the truth, albeit truth tempered by the knowledge and understanding of the child's tolerance for such constructive criticism. Follow Joe Namath's advice that, "if you are afraid of evaluating what you do, if you are dishonest with evaluating what you do, then you are going to have some problems."

You need not resort to false praise to present a positive spin. Ed "Too Tall" Jones's parents helped in him that way: "Of course I experienced coaches yelling at me. But when I went back and explained that to my mom and dad, they always had something positive to say about that. They said, 'Hey, if he doesn't yell at you, he doesn't like you and he doesn't think you have the talent to go to another level.' They said to be concerned when he stops yelling at you."

If a child isn't playing much or at all, you can pick out something that may lift them, while still making it clear that he or she can play an active role in other ways, such as pushing teammates in practice or supporting them in games. You can encourage the child to improve their standing by practicing longer and giving maximum effort, eventually leading to earning the coach's attention and trust and receiving the corresponding rewards.

Whatever you do or say, you should try to stay grounded in reality. It is natural for a parent to be biased about everything his or her child does, or to idealize what the child might become if only this or that. But it is better if you take proper account of the child's actual athletic attributes at the time, from size to speed to coordination to fearlessness, as compared to others on a team or in an age group. It is better if you attempt to keep expectations reasonably achievable.

Sometimes you can do all of this and it doesn't make the situation better. Sometimes a conversation with the child doesn't leave the child feeling comfortable. Sometimes speaking with the coach doesn't leave you feeling comfortable, even if you did frame your concerns in a reasonable, diplomatic, nonthreatening way—a way that makes it clear you care about maintaining or improving the morale and welfare of the entire team and aren't just seeking special favors for one child. In some cases you even may be left with little choice but to speak up to authorities around the team or program.

What if that fails too? What if your concerns are still not heeded or alleviated? What if it still doesn't seem right?

Your instinct might be to entirely remove the child from the situation.

And you might need to act on it.

In that scenario, you can help a child find another team, league, sport, or activity—one you can still find a way to share together. You can still find something that would give a child some enrichment and enjoyment while also strengthening your relationship. That special connection is the one and only thing that the parent should not want to lose.

"So Specialized"

GROWING UP in Miami, Raul Ibanez spent much of his time where many kids, especially Cuban American kids raised on the rich tradition of *beisbol*, spend it.

He spent it in the outfield shagging flies.

He spent it in the batter's box taking hacks.

Did he ever.

"Down there you can play year round," Ibanez said. "So I played all this summer ball. I played in the winter, I played in the spring. I played all the time."

He played little else.

Then in junior high, he simply couldn't play anymore. It was not because he was struggling and not because he was injured.

"I think I kind of had enough," Ibanez said.

So Ibanez sat out for more than two years before rekindling his love for the sport on his own and taking the field for Miami Sunset Senior High, Miami-Dade Community College, and later, for four Major League franchises—still getting something from the game after age forty, and giving plenty too, hitting three critical home runs for the Yankees during the 2012 postseason and twenty-four home runs for the Mariners prior to the 2013 All-Star break.

"You know, more is not better when it comes to playing," Ibanez said. "You've got parents who put their kids in that year-round thing. You've got kids practicing four, five, six days and playing four, five, six games a week. These kids are eight. That's ridiculous. My son will never play that many games at that age."

In this day and age, that will make his son different from many peers. This is the era of hyper-specialization in youth sports, when many parents believe the best or only way for their kids to grow in a sport—and perhaps bring glory and riches to the family—is for the kids to start that sport early and never stop, playing it constantly and exclusively. Parents are also operating in a modern sports environment that normalizes, promotes, and facilitates that way of thinking. It's easy. It's expected. As Cheryl Miller bemoaned, "For us, when we traveled with AAU, you had to fundraise, get out and wash cars, and try to earn your money to do it. Unfortunately in this day and age, kids are being showered with shoes and traveling."

Even the US educational system incentivizes volume over variety because of what it offers to skilled jocks down the line. Australian golf star

Karrie Webb is amazed by what America provides to collegiate athletes "that really isn't offered anywhere else in the world." She said, "Those parents see how much money it will save if they can get a scholarship, and they make their kids use, from a young age, the sport they are the best in. The kids may not like that sport, but it's the one they are best in."

In prematurely narrowing the playing field as such, adults are placing the worst sort of limit on a child. They are limiting the child's exposure to other activities, sporting or otherwise, by pushing the child in that direction or simply leaving no time for anything else. "They could be a great musician, great piano player or guitar player," major league pitcher Tim Hudson said. "But they need to have the opportunity to do it. A lot of parents are narrow-minded; they drive their kids toward one sport."

In doing so, parents put unlimited pressure on a child to succeed in a single endeavor. A chorus of youth sport educators, psychologists, and pediatricians say that is not the ideal approach. The professional athletes we interviewed had even stronger words about it. Many, without provocation, identified specialization as the most rampant, disturbing modern problem in youth sports today. It is what compelled John Smoltz to conclude that youth sports have "changed for the worse. It's too specialized, overuse, overabuse, you name it," Smoltz said. "And the one thing that's saddening is that we're creating little factories, little prodigies, and we're not allowing kids to be kids."

Kids enjoy experimenting, imagining, playing for its sake. When adults try to mold too much too soon, they may go beyond merely encouraging a child's dream. They create unreasonable hopes for a child, hopes the child may not hold him or herself.

"I know a lot of players nowadays who from the time they are eight think they are going to be in the Hall of Fame," Hudson said. "It's not that easy. [Adults] are blowing a lot of smoke up their butts. There has to be some kind of reality there. I think that comes from the parents and the coaches—treating it as a game, treating it as a fun sport, and not treating it as, 'You are eight but you have to make a career out of this, and by the way, there's going to be a lot of pressure.'"

For former Major League pitcher **Al Hrabosky**, the primary source of outrage was the procurement of pitching lessons for seven-year-olds: "Ridiculous." For current Major League pitcher Hudson, it was the nonstop game scheduling for kids near that age: "Crazy."

Athletes from all sports shared the same strong sentiment.

"I hate it," said NFL quarterback **Ryan Fitzpatrick**, who didn't play football until he was eleven and continued doing a little of everything else—soccer, swimming, basketball, baseball, even triathlons—until paring down to basketball and football in high school.

"I hate it when they tell kids to play one sport," said 1993 World Series MVP **Joe Carter**, who enjoyed the chance to participate in football, basketball, baseball, and track before finally choosing baseball over football in college. "I *absolutely* hate it."

Brian Jordan got to make his decision on a sport even later in life. He didn't choose between football and baseball until it was time to turn professional, and then he switched from one to the other. He called himself a "firm believer" in one-sport burnout. "When I talk to kids and parents, I encourage them to play as many sports as they can," Brian Jordan said. "Don't try to specialize on one."

Many parents aren't heeding that advice, or warning.

"Things are so specialized now," Steve Kerr said. "When I was growing up, I played three different sports, and I think there was a healthiness. And the fact that you go from one coach to another, one sport to another, a different set of teammates, you learn different values and different techniques; you use different muscles. Now everybody is playing the same sport year-round, which is great for your skill development, but I think there are more injuries than ever before and there's more burnout. And you lose something in the equation."

One thing that can be lost: innocence.

"I think in today's world we try to create everything for the kids," Jamie Moyer said. "We try to make it happen instead of letting the kids allow it to happen. Let the kids be creative in their own little world."

Moyer, born in 1962, remembers his childhood world differently. He remembers long lazy summers during which "if you could kick it, or throw it, we played it," with the balls of choice being a Spalding, a Wiffle, or a Nerf.

"That's where you learn about yourself, and when you play a lot of sports, I think you get a better idea of what your likes are instead of being forced to play a sport because of the talent levels," Moyer said. "Now it's, 'Well, I gotta have my son or my daughter in their sport.' And what ends up happening is by the time they get to become teenagers, they either have injuries, and some are major injuries based on the sport, or they lose interest. And all of a sudden now at fourteen, fifteen, and sixteen, the parents are upset because their child has lost interest, and because it's been turned into such a job and it really shouldn't be. Your childhood years, your youthful years should be the most fun years of your life."

Instead, schedules are being stuffed with just one activity, day after day, week after week, year after year. **Garrett Anderson**, a three-time Major League All-Star, noted that even while playing as a professional, he didn't play baseball year-round. The kids who do? "I feel sorry for them," he said. "It's too much. Find something else to do; broaden your horizons. You might find something you like better."

For many, there's hardly anything they could like less.

"It will turn the kids into not enjoying the game and then they are not wanting to play it," Hudson said.

Smoltz played baseball and basketball all the way through high school, and almost did the same at Michigan State University before signing with the Detroit Tigers. He had trouble giving either up, let alone both. Still, he understands why kids today feel like giving up everything.

"I think sports are such a great tool, great learning lesson, and we're just zapping them of that," Smoltz said. "There's a study that more kids at the age of thirteen, more kids than ever, are quitting."

They are.

"And no one's paying attention," Smoltz said.

Not, in his view, the coaches or the parents.

"The two go hand in hand," he said.

Some parents are dragging kids to the field by the arm before those arms are even hinting at muscles. Such early specialization has long been accepted in individual sports such as golf, tennis, figure skating, gymnastics, and swimming. In those sports, athletes can reach the highest levels of competition at young ages. Not all of them take that course, however. Twelve-time Olympic swimming medalist **Dara Torres** said playing different sports "chopped up the monotony a little bit."

In recent years, this trend has spread into team sports.

"I see so many kids now, and all they do is play one sport," Shannon Sharpe said. "All they play is baseball, all they play is football, all they play is basketball. Let them play a whole bunch of things. They'll tell you what they like. Don't you decide what they should do because you have this aspiration that you might have the next Tiger Woods or Kobe Bryant or Peyton Manning. Come on."

Former Major League slugger **Fred McGriff** observed, while a high school baseball coach, that "a lot of the guys who played multiple sports, they are good at all of them, and they're not as great at any of them." He found it laughable when parents would come to him and brag about their sons having played 160 games the year before. "It's crazy," McGriff said, smiling. "When I was coming out I probably played thirty or forty games a year."

That light adolescent and teenage slate didn't stop him from hitting 493 Major League home runs.

Chipper Jones is frequently asked by parents whether they should sign their kids up for travel or summer ball, in addition to the standard spring baseball season.

His answer?

"No," Jones said. "You are going to get the kid burned out by the time he is fifteen, sixteen, or seventeen years old. The most games I ever played until I was sixteen years old was twenty-five or thirty, maybe. Once you get to sixteen or seventeen, you are starting to play American Legion ball, you are starting to play summer ball. But the most I played, even then, was probably ninety games. I just think if kids play one hundred games at twelve years old, they get burned out of the game. They need something that rekindles their fire come springtime. Let them play football, even if it's flag football, let them play soccer, let them play hoops—do all of those things, and then that fire is going to be there and they are really going to work at it, whatever the sport."

Rich Gannon played quarterback in the NFL for eighteen years, but he lives in Minnesota, which is known as the state of hockey. "And these poor kids, honestly, they skate year-round. I am talking about six or seven years old, they are in summer hockey," Gannon said. "It's like a vocation for the parents."

Consequently, it can become more like a job for the kids. The parents present—and the kids start to see—no option other than total immersion.

"In other words, if you want to play hockey, then you better be skating year-round or you're not going to get a chance to play in high school," Gannon said. "I think that's unfortunate. I played a lot of different sports, even in high school. Naturally what happens is you're going to gravitate toward what you're best at, what you like the most, what you're more comfortable with."

Tom Glavine grew up in Boston in the 1970s. He played hockey and baseball, and his parents told him that when one sport's season ended, he should put away the equipment and focus on another. No camps. No overlap. "So I had a separation. And I think a lot of kids nowadays don't." Many didn't even in his day. Many of them quit because "it had become a chore for them." Glavine eventually kept going in baseball and became a three-hundred-game winner.

Chad Pennington considers himself similarly fortunate.

"My parents always made sure that I took breaks," the former NFL quarterback said. "I played football and I played basketball, and the summer was my chance to go to the lake and just be a kid. So I always had some nice breaks in there to change it up and not be so monotonous. That's why I truly believe in changing it up and staying away from specialization as much as you can, and letting these kids experience different sports."

What if they are really good, really young at one sport?

Mary Joe Fernandez certainly was. And while she started early, because tennis tends to demand that to some degree, her parents moderated it just enough. She is convinced that made a long-term difference. "My contemporaries were practicing more than me, like [Steffi] Graf and [Gabriella] Sabatini. And they got off to faster starts than I did. But looking back, it kept me grounded and fresh, and I probably played longer because of that."

In team sports, Pennington still sees no reason for kids to start personal training until eighth or ninth grade at the earliest, and he still sees a need for choices.

"They've got plenty of time [later] to focus on it," Pennington said. "Unless it's a sport like gymnastics, where they are young when they are competing in the Olympics or whatever, then it's a different story. But there's only one time in your life, and that's your childhood, where you can play and experience any and every sport. And for the most part, going through their high school years and middle school years, they need to enjoy it."

Sports excess and extremism create many risks. One of those is that the child will go along with it not due to a genuine passion for the sport but because he or she gets the sense that it is what the parent wants; the child fears creating more stress and frustration for the parent. A possible consequence of that is that the child sacrifices self, learning to dismiss or ignore an inner voice in order to please—or at the very least placate—the adult.

Jeff Foster got to play several sports as a kid and was good at some, not so good at others, but he generally got to figure that out on his own. "As long as they love it, they should stick with it," Foster said of a single sport. "My concern is a lot of kids are getting pushed to do stuff they don't necessarily want to do. And how do you tell your parents no?"

Sometimes kids' bodies speak for them.

It's not just the mind and heart that suffer sports burnout.

The shoulders, elbows, and knees can too.

"I don't think you can pick a sport at six," John Smoltz said. "I believe that your body will gravitate to the sport that you'll play. I really do. Maybe I'm wrong. But genetically there's a lot of things that go into a sport. I don't think you can say at eight years old that this is what you're going to do, now start lifting weights."

He's not wrong.

The experts not only agree with him; they go further.

The National Association for Sport and Physical Education (NASAPE) does not recommend that athletes under age fifteen focus on one sport to the exclusion of others, due not only to an interference with "informed decision making since the opportunity to experiment and try another sport has been moved," but also due to "more documented risks because over-training and excessive time commitment to one activity are disruptive." [10]

The American Academy of Pediatrics released a position statement in 2000 and reaffirmed that statement in 2006 and 2010. [11]

10 National Association for Sport and Physical Education. (2010). *Guidelines for participation in youth sport programs: Specialization versus multi-sport participation* [Position statement]. Reston, VA: Author.

11 American Academy of Pediatrics. Committee on Sports Medicine and Fitness, http://www.ncbi.nlm.nih.gov/pubmed/10878168

Their message?

"Children involved in sports should be encouraged to participate in a variety of different activities and develop a wide range of skills. Young athletes who specialize in just one sport may be denied the benefits of varied activity while facing additional physical, physiologic, and [psychological] demands from intense training and competition."

Such training, in the view of the committee, "can lead to short- and long-term health consequences."

These relate to the stress that repetitive activity places on bones and joints. In 2012, Tommy John, a former Major League pitcher who is the namesake for the revolutionary elbow surgery that has extended many professionals' careers, stood up on behalf of younger athletes. He joined the STOP Sports Injuries Campaign, which was launched two years earlier by the American Orthopaedic Society for Sports Medicine. John enlisted in order to "highlight that playing all year long is not going to make you a better player and may cause long-term injuries. I played basketball and baseball when I was growing up, which I know helped me develop my skills and muscles both on and off the field and on many different levels."[12] STOP cited a ten-year study, published in the *American Journal of Sports Medicine*, that linked innings pitched in youth and adolescent baseball to serious injury. John recommended that kids adhere to Little League Baseball pitch limits and urged parents to recognize that "very few kids make it to the college level to play baseball and even fewer make it to the big leagues."

Smoltz, who successfully rebounded from Tommy John surgery during his Major League career, pointed to another issue that very young pitchers face. "If you just throw a baseball over and over and over again, and you don't do other things, you're going to underdevelop your body," Smoltz said. "That balance is so important, for your body to be well-rounded."

---

12   STOP Sports Injuries Campaign press release, July 24, 2012.

It's not just pitchers who can benefit from other activities either, though that's what Tim Hudson has done best during his Major League career. Hitters can too. "Baseball is such a one-sided dominant sport," Hudson said. "You are constantly throwing; you are constantly swinging. If you don't play other sports, you don't have the opportunity to develop the other parts of your body evenly."

That development is necessary for an athlete to really excel at anything. That's why Pennington argued that, even in terms of pure athletic development—to say nothing of the emotional elements— diversification has inherent benefits.

Especially at an early age.

"If you are playing all kinds of different sports, that is where you are going to get your agility, your hand-eye coordination," Pennington said. "That is where is you learn about the little things, while you are still having fun."

The baseball players just playing baseball?

"They are not becoming better athletes," Ibanez said. "They are becoming better at one thing."

Brian Jordan noted, "When you play different sports, you use different muscles. Balance, your core, your athletic ability is much better off when you can do more than one sport."

Tiki Barber wrestled in junior high.

"And it was maybe the most valuable thing that I did outside of preparing for the game, because it taught me about my body," the New York Giants all-time rushing leader said. "I learned a skill, wrestling, that would seemingly have no benefit to football, but it had a huge benefit to me. Same thing with running track and learning a discipline of how to run and sprint. You never know what skills you are going to pick up from another sport."

Roy Hibbert learned something about his body early on, while he looked down upon his classmates. "I was always tall," Hibbert said. And so some things on the basketball court came easy, such as blocking shots and grabbing rebounds. The other sports? They never felt as natural. Still, even now as an NBA All-Star center who stands seven feet, two inches, Hibbert wishes he had given soccer, baseball, and football more of a go. "I think that would have helped me with foot speed and everything like that," he said. "Don't specialize. Look at LeBron; he played football. Let kids play a plethora of sports. You learn a lot from everything you do. And then, as they get older, kids can single them out or whittle them down to the one they want to play."

The odds are stacked against your child ever turning pro in a particular sport, no matter the number of practice hours. "What is it, one in one hundred thousand make it to the top level?" Jonathan Ogden asked. "You're not looking for that. You're looking to utilize sports as a way to get better at life."

Depending on how you define "top," the odds are even worse than that.

"As you grow and get better, you start realizing, especially as you get in the high school and college ranks, 'Pro ball, maybe that's a possibility,'" Tim Hudson said. "But it's not for everybody. Every single parent thinks their kid is going to be the next big thing, and that's just not reality. And eventually that's going to be very disappointing for the kid."

The athletes we interviewed for this book didn't suffer that disappointment. They all beat the odds to some degree. Still, for some that may not have happened had they been limited early on and steered down a single sporting path. It might surprise you to learn how many of them were initially more involved with, and devoted to, something different than the athletic endeavor in which they would make their names. If they had focused solely on that "first love" through childhood and adolescence, they may have never learned that their skill set and temperament translated better to something else.

And that, as Brian Jordan noted, they "could have been better at another sport."

"Now you have kids six, seven years old, and they are being told to pick one sport, and it may not be their sport," Joe Carter said. "They don't know what kind of athlete they are going to be."

Carter, who hit 396 home runs in sixteen Major League seasons, expressed concern about what he sees occurring in the African American community in particular, where adults are steering their kids to just one or two of the sports currently considered the most glamorous: football and basketball.

"We've lost a lot of baseball players," Carter said.

Matt Kemp had the talent to go the basketball route, but he also kept the baseball option open.

"Look what he's doing," Carter said.

In 2011 Kemp finished second in National League MVP voting.

Certainly, all that time in basketball didn't hurt his baseball development.

In many cases, one sport can help with another.

Al Hrabosky frequently experienced struggles in baseball as a kid, getting cut from three youth league teams as well as an eighth-grade squad. But he kept trying. And during that period, he also kept playing football. "My football mentality really helped me as a baseball player," said Hrabosky, now a St. Louis Cardinals broadcaster. While he didn't pitch for his high school team until his senior year, he eventually made that a thirteen-year Major League career during which he saved ninety-seven games. And that football mentality earned him the nickname, the Mad Hungarian.

Denis Potvin grew up in Quebec and followed an unconventional Canadian sporting path, especially considering his older brother Jean's success in hockey.

Denis played baseball.

"Loved it," he said.

Denis played lacrosse.

"Loved it," he said.

Denis played football.

"My dream was to play for UCLA in the Rose Bowl," he said. "Thank goodness that didn't happen."

What he loved most? The contact.

"And maybe that's what I brought to the ice," he said.

He brought that football mentality, the lacrosse agility, and the baseball dexterity to junior hockey and then the New York Islanders during a Hall of Fame hockey career.

Jason Witten, the Pro Bowl NFL tight end, understands the mindset: "Kids think, 'Hey, if I spend time year-round on this deal, I'll be that much better. And not wasting time swinging a baseball bat if I'm a football player.'"

Yet he watches his quarterback with the Dallas Cowboys, Tony Romo, making balletic moves in and out of the pocket, and he sees evidence of Romo's basketball background. "And to compete in anything, that [versatility is] the most important trait an athlete can have," Witten said. "Sometimes we forget that, because kids are so focused on one sport."

Earlier Kerr mentioned the use of "different muscles" as a benefit to trying different sports. But it's more than just muscles. It's your mind too.

"Steve Nash is a much better basketball player because he played soccer," said Kerr, who was the GM of the Phoenix Suns during some of the time Nash spent there. "The angles, the vision … if he hadn't played soccer, I don't know if he'd be as good a point guard."

Certainly Jay Feely wouldn't have been as solid a kicker. Feely played several sports through eighth grade, and then football and soccer competitively in high school while still playing the others on the side.

"I want my kids to play everything," Feely said. "My son's doing gymnastics, football, golf, baseball, and soccer. And whatever he wants to do, whatever he enjoys the most, that's what he is going to do."

For now, Jace Feely is good at just about everything.

Jace's older sister, Alexandra?

"Not a great athlete," Feely said. "We've tried soccer, a bunch of different things. Then we found swimming. She's not great at it, but she likes it. And it gives her an identity, and no one else does it in our family—it's just hers. So it's perfect for her. She's got friends, so I'm happy."

And that has plenty of value, even if Alexandra never comes close to wearing a medal around her neck. As former athletes know better than anyone, it pays to let your kid dive into something different and, occasionally, take a pause from diving into anything at all.

"A Totally Different Perspective"

BRETT HULL wasn't merely the son of a hockey player.

He was the son of a hockey legend.

Bobby Hull was known as "the Golden Jet" for his blazing speed and blond hair. The ice was home for the Hull family, with Bobby's brother Dennis also starring in the NHL and Bobby's children finding comfort there. Michelle, his daughter, was a competitive figure skater as a child, and his sons, Bobby Jr. and Blake, rose to the junior and senior ranks, while Bart ultimately played in the hockey minor leagues after his Canadian Football League career.

Among Bobby's kids, however, Brett was the one blessed with the most talent.

Did he ever feel pushed toward the family tradition?

"No," Brett said. "Never from him."

From the outside world?

"Yes," Brett said. "But never from my dad, never from him. His theory was: If you are going to play, you are committed. Do it to the best of your ability. Give it 110 percent."

Brett's ability rivaled that of anyone in the game. By the time Brett was finished, he and Bobby would be known as hockey's most fearsome father-son combination, the first combination to ever win the Hart Trophy (Most Valuable Player) and Lady Byng Trophy (sportsmanship), and the first combination to each have a jersey number retired by at least one NHL team. Yet Bobby passed on more than athletic gifts to Brett at birth or sage hockey advice to him through the years. He passed on a supportive approach that Brett carried forward to his own kids. At his Hall of Fame speech, Brett spoke of how proud he was of his son Jude's maturity and passion, even if Jude had chosen a slightly different method of athletic expression, stopping pucks rather than shooting them. "I'm not sure where it happened, but between your great-uncle Dennis and your grandpa and me, we have 1,654 goals ... and you're a goalie."

Grant Hill, like Brett Hull, was exposed to sports early.

How couldn't he be?

"I was closer to professional sports than most kids, with my father being in them," Hill said.

That understates Calvin's prominence. By the time Grant was born in 1972, the Yale graduate already had an NFL Offensive Rookie of the Year and had become one of the most prominent players on "America's team," carrying the ball for the Dallas Cowboys. Grant carried that family name but not the corresponding burdens, not feeling the pressure to outdo his father inside the house or out. And when Grant ultimately went into sports, he wasn't expected to mirror his schedule after that of a pro athlete.

Not like many schedules do today.

"Yeah, we had tournaments on weekends and practices throughout the week, but you didn't feel like anybody was pushing you," Hill said. "Now it's so organized and so serious that I think kids rebel against that.

Kids want to find themselves and want to learn from experiences. And we've sort of failed them in a sense, where it becomes almost a job."

Hill's first daughter, Myla, took to soccer early on her own. When she was seven, she was advanced enough to play on a travel team as well as a local team. Grant's wife, Tamia, ruled against it. "She said, 'I can't have two professional athletes in the family,'" Hill said. "It's too much."

That's a decision Jamal Mashburn, himself the son of a boxer, made about basketball travel leagues when it came to his second son, even though Jamal Jr. was "pretty good."

"What's the purpose of him traveling to Jacksonville [from Miami Beach] at nine years old?" Mashburn said. "To me it doesn't make sense."

Darren Collison's parents, Dennis and June, were elite track stars, representing the cooperative republic of Guyana in the Pan American Games and Olympics, respectively.

Through them, he said, "I just fell in love with sports in general."

Yet they didn't put him on the fast track to one particular sport or another. That meant he could play football, baseball, and basketball, even though the latter would have seemed like a longshot endeavor for him due to his relatively diminutive stature.

"Being the smallest one on the court every single time was really hard for me," Collison said. "I was able to overcome that when I understood how to use my speed and quickness. And being small wasn't a bad thing; it was actually a good thing."

Eventually, after years of imitating similarly short but quick players such as Allen Iverson, he followed these players into the NBA, and is now an established professional point guard. But that all came after his parents allowed him to do his own thing.

It's one thing for us, as observers, to explain the value of a varied, unforced, and unencumbered youth sports experience. It's quite another if those sentiments come from those who know best what worked for them and what didn't when they were kids. That, again, is why we asked athletes to share their experiences, and used them throughout the book. And in some cases, we provided a peek at what they're doing with their own kids.

We wanted to know how elite athletes chose to proceed as youth sports parents. That's why we asked the children of athletes to share their stories, as Hull, Hill, and Collison did above. That's why we solicited more detail about their own practical applications of their philosophies and prescriptions. These are the people who know the score because they have been through the process themselves. They know the proper place of the parent, and they know the appropriate limits in terms of competition, single-sport participation, parental involvement, and intensity.

"Athletes like us have a totally different perspective than the average fan," said **John Offerdahl**, a five-time NFL Pro Bowl selection. "I don't know many athletes at our level that really put a lot of pressure on their kids to perform. I think that's very different than the average person who may have played high school ball and have higher aspirations."

"I have a daughter, and I never said one word to her like, 'You should try track and field' or 'You should try sports,'" former Olympic hurdler Bob Beamon said.

Tim Brown, a Heisman Trophy winner and one of the NFL's all-time leading receivers, has gone so far as to adopt a policy with his son that he resented when his mother enforced upon him. Josephine thought Tim was too small to play football, so he had his father, Eugene, sign the permission papers. "She thought I was practicing for the band," Brown said. "So it was the only way I got in."

Now Tim Jr. wants in at age nine.

"Dying to play," Brown said.

Brown won't let him.

"One, I think he'll get burned out," Brown said. "Two, I don't think the coaching at that level is proper. They are not teaching good techniques. Consequently, these kids are hitting like the guys in the NFL are hitting right now and knocking people out, and knocking themselves out."

Certainly you can find a few exceptions to this train of thought—athletic parents who are pushing some rather than pulling back.

Jerry Stackhouse was the youngest of eleven children from a working-class family. He beat the odds to win a national high school basketball championship at Oak Hill Academy, star at the University of North Carolina, and fill primary and then secondary roles during an NBA career of nearly two decades. He's also a father to three kids, and he became so involved with Jaye's AAU basketball team that he moved five of Jaye's teammates into the house to give them a better situation and more hope, especially scholastically. He believes in affection but also discipline for those coming from homes where these things are often absent. Sometimes he will say no just to give those kids a reality check.

Stackhouse has shot especially straight with Jaye, who is not only a member of the National Honor Society but also a prep phenom in football and basketball in Atlanta. Stackhouse spoke of recognizing the "fine line" between not expecting his kids "to trail my path, but at the same time, get the most out of what you are capable of."

And Jaye?

"He's an athlete," Stackhouse said. "He's got a chance in a couple of sports, in football and basketball. So I am going to push him. I think he wants the push. You see it from him; you can feel whether they want it or not, and that's when you've got to know whether to push harder or back off a little bit. So right now, I'm going to push it as long as he wants it, and that's where we're at."

This all comes back to the communication we have discussed throughout the book, and parents using it to measure the thickness of a child's skin.

In this case Stackhouse chose the "tough love" approach, even though his interaction with Jaye comes with another complication: Jaye is the product of a previous relationship. As a result, Stackhouse may see sports one way, and Jaye's mother "may be looking at it a whole different way. It's different dynamics, so you've got to pray about it."

Personal reflection may be more necessary than prayer.

"We are human," Stackhouse said. Stackhouse admits to an "episode" during which he railed upon Jaye for a couple of careless turnovers at the end of a game. It was done in a way he would never criticize another kid.

"But because he is mine, I think I can," Stackhouse said. "He responded."

Stackhouse then referred back to the original premise of the interview, whether parents have become too overbearing.

"I might be that guy you are talking about a little bit," he said, laughing.

Tim Hardaway Sr. may have been that guy too. Then, as the earlier anecdote revealed, he eventually realized his error. He realized what Jamie Moyer related earlier: that a child's experience is unique and independent from what the parent experienced as a child, and the child's reaction to any particular event or style of instruction may be different as well.

You might argue that accomplished athletes would find it easier to pull back with their own kids, because there is less reason to live vicariously through them. You would have good reason to think that. These fathers or mothers already made it in sports, so there are fewer feelings of regret. Being an elite athlete tends to come with some financial comfort, so long as that fortune isn't squandered; that can create less of a compulsion to push a kid simply to improve a family's standing. And as Offerdahl and Hull mentioned, children of athletes can feel pressure from outsiders to emulate the exploits of their parents, and so the "last thing I need to do is put pressure on them."

Athletes know better than anyone how unproductive and unhealthy that pressure can be, especially at a young age, because some of them felt or witnessed its effects during their own athletic ascents.

Still, athletes have one thing working against them: they know how something *should* be done. That requires them to exercise even more restraint than the average parent. That can be a challenge even for an exceptional parent, such as Allan Houston, the National Fatherhood Initiative's 2007 Father of the Year. Even Houston has had to dance a bit when his son Allan Wade III has participated in his father-child basketball retreats in New York City. It's been a test to work "with that dynamic of coaching him in a group. There is a fine line between correcting him, letting him have fun, encouraging him, but also letting him be part of a group."

Charles Johnson, the former Major League catcher, dealt with this when his son Beau was playing baseball at age eight. "I have all this information in my head, but I [am] at a point where I have to hold back on what I want to tell him so he can understand it." That meant telling Beau just to see the ball and hit the ball. Instructions about reading the pitcher's release? That would have to come later.

The idea is not to steer too much, especially at young ages. Not to one sport. Not to one position. Not to one way of practicing, or performing. It is better to expand options, horizons, and ambitions than to narrow.

This, again, is something that elite athletes understand more than most.

"You have to let them become what they are going to become first," Dwyane Wade said. "Just because you want your kid to play something doesn't mean necessarily that is in their nature, or that they are going to be able to play it."

This can be true even if a kid *wants* to play something, like Tim Brown's nephew wanted to play football when he was twelve. He wanted to be like his uncle. "And when he got hit in the mouth, that was the last time he ever played," Brown said. "You are born to play football or not."

A child may not be born to play a certain, or any, sport, even if he or she might be expected to possess those talents and inclinations due to his or her bloodlines. Chipper Jones has four sons; three play sports and "one has no athletic ability." Dan Marino, arguably the greatest passer of all-time, had a couple of his sons in athletic "situations where they weren't successful."

So what did he do? Keep squeezing square pegs into round holes?

"I took them out of there," Marino said. "You know, at a young age it is tough. It can ruin their image of the sport. So it is a hard line; it is a hard to decide, but the thing is to find what they like, and then you can push them that way."

One of Offerdahl's sons chose baseball; the other chose John's sport of football. Offerdahl said he didn't lean on his sons to do either, not like his two older sisters leaned on him to play football rather than volleyball. If he has pressured his kids, including his daughter, to do anything outside of school, it was piano or something like that, something that expanded their horizons beyond sports.

Here's another reality: even if kids do inherit some athletic gifts, they may not want to do exactly the same things with them.

This is something Herschel Walker learned from his son Christian. When just six, Christian was already the fastest kid in Texas up through age twelve. He seemed to be following exactly in the speedy footsteps of his famous father, who was a two-time All-American track star at the University of Georgia, while also winning a Heisman Trophy. At the end of the school year, Christian told Herschel he didn't want to run anymore.

"He decided he wanted to be a gymnast," Walker said. "I didn't want to tell him he is going to be too big or whatever. I believe if he wants to do this, he'll be the first six-foot, 1,220-pound person doing the iron crawls. Instead of pushing a kid to do what you want them to do, let a kid find his own way."

Tony Dorsett did that with his son Anthony, who dreamed of becoming plenty of things when he was young: doctor, lawyer, scientist.

His father had just nodded at all of his activities and ambitions, in the way Dorsett did for his two youngest daughters playing soccer and his oldest daughter, Jazz, playing basketball, which would lead her to a scholarship at Oklahoma State, before she left to pursue a fashion career. His primary concern with all of his kids was simply that if they chose a sport, regardless of which one it was, they were put in environments where there was a premium on "learning how to do it" rather than being screamed into it. It just so happened that Anthony found his way to the NFL, playing eight seasons at defensive back.

Chris Mullin has three sons and a daughter. In guiding his children toward their activities or sports of choice, Mullin drew upon his own experience and his belief that if he hadn't learned to shoot the way he did, "I don't know if I would keep playing" basketball.

"At some point, you've got to get something back," Mullin said. "You've got to make a shot. Otherwise I would go to tennis or swimming."

So when his oldest son, Sean, chose to cradle rather than bounce a ball, Mullin went with it. Sean eventually earned a spot on the Bryant University lacrosse team.

"You have to have a passion for it," Mullin said. "If there's no passion for it, it's going to die down, no matter how good you are. And sometimes the better you are, the passion goes away quicker if you are not enjoying it. Because you get put under a microscope; you are getting judged, and you are getting compared to other people."

Including a famous father.

"If you don't truly love the sport, it's going to wear out," Mullin said.

Mullin's second son, Christopher Jr., not only shared his father's love for basketball at the start, but also sustained that love by "getting enough back" from it as a child, in the form of progress and achievement. Chris Jr. was too young at the time of his father's career to process much of it, but he learned to deal with the microscope on him as a result of his father's achievement, one that zoomed in as he had more success. He has credited his father for teaching him everything a son could possibly learn about the game, yet he has still found ways to carve out his own niche. His speedier style started attracting the attention of college recruiters when he was just a high school sophomore.

Maybe someday Chris Jr. will get a chance to play against Nick Kerr in the NCAA Tournament. Nick, the son of former NBA player and general manager and current TNT analyst Steve Kerr, had the best of all worlds as a kid. Was it tough being the son of one of basketball's top shooters, especially when that's also your own primary skill? Steve doesn't think so.

"He understands it," Steve said. "[NBA coach] Doug Collins gave me great advice: remind him the perks far outweigh the downside. The tickets, the going to the game, meeting Michael Jordan, that's worth dealing with a few catcalls from the stands. My son has a great attitude about it."

Steve's son benefited from the supportive approach that, as we noted earlier, Steve borrowed from his late father, Malcolm. In a 2009 interview with MaxPreps.com, Nick said, "It's been way better than good. It's all been great. Never have felt any pressure. Never felt like I had to play basketball because my dad did. I just loved to do it and learned by watching him. I'll ask him things from time to time, or once in a while he'll give me a pointer or two, but I think we're just like any other father and son."

Just as Steve and Maddie Kerr, the latter a volleyball player at Cal-Berkeley, are like every father and daughter.

But, in truth, no parent-child relationship is exactly like any other. Every situation requires its own special attention and care.

Brandi Chastain's son Jaden is just six.

When will he play organized sports like his mother? And which one? Or ones?

"I've been asked that question since the time he's been two or three or four," Chastain said. "He loves science and he loves art. I don't know if he is going to play sports. But I am going to introduce him to sports, because I know the value of teamwork and practice and being organized. I don't know if he'll love sports the way I do, but he is competitive. He's outer limits on the competitiveness; I know he has that going for him. It will be my job to temper that passion and emotion in him."

Cliff Floyd felt strong emotions when his young son first started taking a liking to sports. He felt excitement about the future, and the prospect of Tobias' potential. And he felt a tug, from his past, a reminder that he should exercise care and caution, wishing to be the same sort of quiet, calming influence that his own father was.

"I think any dad would hope that a son is better than you," Floyd said. "But I am not going to push him to be anything other than he can be."

If this book pushes you in any direction, let it take you that way.

INDEX

Interviewed Athletes

Track and Field

Volleyball